Your daughter Fanny

Your daughter Fanny

THE
WAR LETTERS
OF FRANCES CLUETT, VAD

Edited by
Bill Rompkey and Bert Riggs

Flanker Press Ltd.
St. John's, NL
2006

Library and Archives Canada Cataloguing in Publication

Cluett, Frances, 1883-1969.
   Your Daughter, Fanny : the war letters of Frances Cluett, VAD / edited by
Bill Rompkey and Bert Riggs.

ISBN 1-894463-92-7

   1. Cluett, Frances 1883-1969--Correspondence. 2. Voluntary aid detach-
ments--Correspondence. 3. World War, 1914-1918--Hospitals--France--Rouen. 4.
World War, 1914-1918--Personal narratives, Canadian. I. Riggs, Bertram G., 1954-
II. Rompkey, William, 1936- III. Title.

D640.C58 2006   940.4'7642092   C2006-903966-6

PRINTED IN CANADA

FLANKER PRESS
P.O. BOX 2522, STATION C
ST. JOHN'S, NL, CANADA A1C 6K1
TOLL FREE: 1-866-739-4420
WWW.FLANKERPRESS.COM

Battlefield cover image: Captain H. E. Knobel. Department of National Defence.
Library and Archives Canada. PA-001020.

Cover Design by

First Canadian edition printed August 2006

10 9 8 7 6 5 4 3 2 1

We acknowledge the financial support of: the Government of Canada through the
Book Publishing Industry Development Program (BPIDP); the Canada Council for
the Arts which last year invested $20.0 million in writing and publishing through-
out Canada; the Government of Newfoundland and Labrador, Department of
Tourism, Culture and Recreation.

Ours is a glorious heritage, handed down to us by our forefathers, as trustees for our descendants; and it is our duty to give it into their care inviolate, and unbroken.

Vincent Cluett
July 1914

Written while Vincent Cluett was a student at Bishop Feild College, St. John's, this excerpt is from an essay entitled "Newfoundland's Duty to the Empire," which won the St. Catherine's (Ontario) Chapter of the IODE Prize, and received special mention among all the essays written by a large number of school students in Canada and other parts of the Empire.

PREFACE

One of the absolute joys of being an archivist is receiving an unexpected telephone call, letter, email, or visit from someone who has a small treasure trove of personal papers for which they are looking for a home. Such was the case in the winter of 1993 when the Rev. Vernon Cluett wrote to tell me about the letters his aunt, Frances Cluett of Belleoram, had written home to her mother during World War I. He was wondering if the archives at Memorial University's Queen Elizabeth II Library would be interested in giving them a permanent home. The answer was a definitive "yes!"

Before long, two packages, the first containing the letters and other paper documents, the second a worn photograph album with more than one hundred prints, arrived at the archives, where they have remained ever since. They were made ready for use by our researchers and have become one of the most important and frequently used bodies of material in our holdings documenting Newfoundland women and the War.

There are thirty-one letters—twenty-eight addressed to Fanny's mother, Matilda, and three to her sister Lil. One of the latter is from 1908 and is included here because it is a long and newsy letter that provides a great deal of context for those that follow, introducing family members and friends in Belleoram, many of whom appear in the War letters. All have been reproduced here, as have four postcards, three to her mother and one to Lil. There is also a short telegram she received from St.

John's on October 2, 1916 bearing the message—"Expect you this week"—a signal that her life would never be the same.

Given the long periods of time between certain letters (none from April to November 1918 and only three from 1919 and one from 1920), it is safe to assume that some did not survive the ravages of time. Those that have, however, provide a true, concise, and compassionate account of a woman at war. We are most fortunate that they are available to provide a genuine and personal snapshot of what life was like in the casualty hospitals of England and France during those years of slaughter that we call World War I and the toll that it took on the women who worked there.

The images that accompany this volume were selected to give faces and definition to the people and places mentioned in some of the letters. They are integral to her story, framing it in the stillness of time. That story now becomes our story, part of the collective memory of a period in our history that we must never be allowed to forget.

Bert Riggs
July 2006

INTRODUCTION

In the First World War, the Great War, Newfoundland men went overseas to fight for King and Country. They slogged through the slime and muck of the trenches, endured the unforgivable circumstances into which they were thrown by the errors of the high command, showed unmatchable valour on the front lines in various theatres of war, gave until the last full measure in quantity and quality far above most other regiments. These were men; stout-hearted men. But what of Newfoundland women? Among those who contributed to the war effort surely those of the VAD (Voluntary Aid Detachment) also saw with their own eyes the same heart of darkness if from a different perspective. For some, like Frances Cluett, staffed the hospitals and the convalescent homes, they tended the sick and the maimed that often overtaxed the wards of Gallipoli and France and London. Others drove ambulances, etc. They experienced the blood and gore in the ultimate result, they experienced the horror through the shortened and immeasurably altered lives of the victims of war. They experienced the unspeakable sadness of promising young lives snuffed out, of young voices stilled forever. And like the men they showed their own kind of strength and determination, their own kind of valour, their own devotion to duty leavened with their own particular fortitude and humour. Far too little has been spoken of them. In her own words this is the story of one of those women, surely a model for all of them. Hopefully this will help to rectify the imbalance.

BELLEORAM AND THE CLUETTS

I met Fanny Cluett only once. It was at the northwest door of the Anglican Cathedral some years ago after the funeral of a Belleoram native. It was a cold, wet, blustery day, as it so often is in St. John's; not a day to tarry long on the sidewalk. She was dressed in a long beige coat with matching hat and held her umbrella against the wind and rain. She carried herself with confidence and self-assurance. She had a presence which I have carried in my mind for many years. "You manage to get to all the funerals, Willy," she said to my father. He was a former student of Fanny, and as a young man in Belleoram had been deeply involved in St. Lawrence Church as church warden and superintendent of the Sunday school. For some years after we moved to St. John's he had been the Diocesan Synod (governing church body of laymen and clergy) representative for Belleoram and one of his responsibilities, one of his duties that he performed without fail, was saying farewell to those of the Belleoram diaspora in St. John's.

That responsibility of caring for your own was one Frances Cluett understood and shared. All her life, both in Belleoram and overseas, she looked after her own as well as others. In particular she cared for Vernon Cluett, to whom we are indebted for the preservation of the letters and photos and for depositing them in the Archives and Manuscripts Division at Memorial University's Queen Elizabeth II Library. Vernon's mother died in childbirth and his older sister, Margaret, the wife of Arthur Cluett, Fanny's brother, took him into their household. Unfortunately Margaret (née Dominix) died of tuberculosis when she was just thirty-six. Vernon was eleven years old at the time. Arthur, with the help of Fanny, was then his guardian. Brother and sister cared for the young man who went on to train at Queen's College and to serve admirably a number of Anglican parishes both in Newfoundland and in Nova Scotia. In later years Fanny took care of her brother until his death and then remained in the old homestead until her own death in 1969.

Belleoram in the early decades of the twentieth century was a society where that kind of caring was the norm, where it was expected of you, where it was second nature.

Belleoram is tucked away on the western side of Fortune Bay on the south coast of Newfoundland. The French used the harbour extensively during the eighteenth century and referred to the place as Bande de Laurier (variations: Bande de l'Arier; Bande de l'Arriere; Bande de la Rier; Bandelore). They were forced to leave the area by the provisions of the Treaty of Utrecht (1713) after which English settlers moved in, referring to it as Belorme's Place after a French adventurer who is believed to have wintered there for twenty years in the latter part of the seventeenth century. It is believed that more settlers arrived shortly after that date and that a small but thriving community, mostly from the southwest of England and the Channel Islands, had developed by 1800. By 1836, the year of the first Newfoundland census, there were 104 people living in Belleoram.

The community is about thirty miles by sea from Grand Bank on the Burin peninsula, about 265 miles from St. John's and about 160 miles from Port aux Basques. The town is set on a rugged peninsula between Hermitage and Fortune Bays, surrounded by rich, dark granite mountains with deep green valleys. It rests snugly in the lee of high hills, its natural harbour sheltered by a gravel spit, "the beach," which acts as a breakwater. The settlement, like so many others in Fortune Bay, developed with the herring fishery. Until the 1890s the economy depended heavily on the selling of herring as bait to American and French fishing fleets. Naturally, The Bait Act of 1884, which prohibited this, caused a great deal of hardship. In 1891 J. Penney and Son built a wharf and a herring store in Belleoram and exported split herring to Halifax until 1899 when a lack of herring and decreased demand put an end to it. The herring industry later increased with the demand by the banking fleet for bait, but declined in the 1930s with the decline of the bank fishery. A short revival of the industry took place in the 1940s and 1950s but by 1970 it was practically non-existent.

The bank fishery and the lobster fishery were once important factors in the economy of Belleoram. The bank fishery reached its peak in 1908 when eighteen vessels with crews totalling 282 men sailed to the lucrative grounds. The abandonment of the fishery by Harvey and

Company in the 1930s and the introduction of steam-powered trawlers helped to bring about the community's decline in the early 1940s. In 1901 there were eleven factories in Belleoram involved in the canning of lobsters and employing twenty-eight men and eleven women. But local canning ceased in the 1930s when Maritime Packers began to buy fresh lobsters.

In the early 1900s the Penneys sold their business to Harvey and Company. This latter company had earlier begun operating a fleet of fishing vessels and a fleet of foreign traders. It terminated its operations in the community in 1937 when it sold to R. Drake. The firm of J. M. Fudge operated a herring packing business in the 1940s and '50s but it went out of business in the early 1960s. Two other established Belleoram firms, W. A. Burdock and Son and Kearley Brothers, as well as several smaller firms, went out of business during the 1940s and '50s.

Like so many others on the island of Newfoundland, Belleoram, from its early years, was a community dominated by fish merchants. In the early decades of the twentieth century, the two biggest firms were the St. John's–based Harvey and Company and Kearleys. Both Kearleys and Cluetts built some of their own ships in Belleoram, thereby developing such local fishing skippers as John Marshall Fudge, Steve Vatcher Cluett, Johnnie Brinton, Gabriel Fudge, Jack Dodge, John Lavhey, Harry Pope, and Ralph Skinner from St. Jacques. During the era of the bankers Harvey's also had a fleet of three-masted (tern) schooners that carried dried fish to their markets in Europe. Very prominent in operating these ships were the Keepings, especially Captain Ben and his son Reginald, and Captain George Kearley. Reg Keeping, while only eighteen years of age, took command of a vessel after the skipper had been washed overboard, and safely completed to the voyage to Oporto. The song, "The John Harvey" tells the story of the loss of this vessel under the command of Captain Kearley, on Cape Gaborus, Nova Scotia, and the rescue of the rest of the crew by John Foote of Belleoram who swam ashore with a rope but who himself died of exposure.

Some merchants imported supplies from Nova Scotia as well as from the "Boston States" (a sort of nickname given to the eastern states of the US including New England and New York). Indeed, the south coast was the area of the Island most independent of St. John's. During the nineteenth century, residents had shown their independence by continuing to sell bait to foreign bankers, a practice which St. John's tried constantly to frustrate. Thus, while on the east coast both the export and import trades had fallen into the hands of foreign and St. John's–based steamship companies, on the southwest coast local schooners continued to ply both the Caribbean and Mediterranean salt fish markets and to return with supplies. But although the ties with Nova Scotia were close, the people of Belleoram were Newfoundlanders, not Canadians. For the Island identity by this time was very strong, and Fanny in her letters resents being taken for a Canadian as did the soldiers of the Newfoundland Regiment.

By and large the society of Belleoram was egalitarian. Tom Kearley was an important merchant in the community, importing and exporting on his own schooners, and carrying on a lucrative local retail enterprise in the community. The young men of the community would often gather in the centre of the village in the evening and go for a walk. Although Kearley was an older man, sometimes they would end up at his house where an intense game of cards would ensue with perhaps a few glasses of cheer, although Kearley himself was not a drinking man. Social life seemed to cross age and station. In addition to the church, the Loyal Orange Lodge and the Society of United Fishermen were community centres. At Christmas these two fraternal societies put on their annual "time," organized a parade through the town, as well as a church service and in the evening a supper and dance in their respective lodges. The "times" were the social event of the year and the talk of the town for many days afterwards, especially the comical episodes. Of course, mummers would be out in force during the season. It was also a time for caring for the less fortunate in the community. My father tells of loading a sleigh at Christmas with food and clothing for those in the community whom life had not served well.

But the church was still the focal point for the community as it had been for many years. Bishop Jones in 1901 reports that he held daily prayers from Friday to Monday which were well-attended as were all the services on Sunday. The clergy (the community was overwhelmingly Church of England, although a small Congregationalist flock was served by Rev. MacDermott from Pool's Cove) were looked upon with great respect: they promoted and supervised education, often arranged for assistance for the unfortunate and sometimes acted as quasi-doctors, even though they may have had a minimum of medical training. Family prayers were common in the community and the whole family was expected to participate.

The church was clearly the focal point of Fanny's life along with her family and her community. She was faithful to the Church of England before she went overseas and while she was there. Before going she had been a leader and an organizer, as her early letters show, caring for the children and the elderly and enjoying their company. And while she was in training and at the Front she tried to attend church whenever she could, reporting to her mother in detail on the hymns and the sermons, as well as on the contrasts between church architecture and manners at home and abroad. The horror of war never seemed to shake her devotion to the church or her attachment to it. Like her letters to family and friends it was her touchstone, her anchor in the storms of life and the horrors of war.

Yet Fanny was a woman of great personal strength who was clearly a leader abroad during her years with the VAD. She had come from a family of leaders and developers. The Cluetts had made a significant contribution to Belleoram from its earliest years. John Cluett of Dorchester was the first English settler in the community in the early nineteenth century. He built a house at the bottom of the harbour under the shadow of the hills, a house which still stands and which has become the town museum. Three marriages blessed John Cluett with thirteen children, most of whom were male, so that his contribution to the population was quite substantial. Three sons, Arthur, Levi, and John inherited a great deal of gear and used it to enhance the family prosperity. Other early family names were Kearley, Dicks, Rose, Dollemont, Scott, and Fudge. Later there would be Burdocks, Banfields, Savourys, Whatleys, Tulks, Lees, and Taylors. Lovell's Directory of 1871 lists two planters[1] who had come from Nova Scotia, John and Jacob Romkey.[2] The latter was my great-grandfather.

It was John Cluett who at his own expense built the first school in Belleoram in the 1830s. Evidently the education was to be of a very high standard. In 1849 the inspector reports that the first class was fully examined in reading, spelling, writing, and ciphering and acquitted themselves with much credit. In the 1890s geography was added to the curriculum. As early as 1810 one could obtain a diploma equivalent to a high-school education and a second mate's ticket in navigation. So Fanny Cluett would have graduated from the then equivalent of high school, perhaps more like the O levels of an English grammar school, with a sound education absorbed from British teachers. It was to stand her in good stead when she returned to teaching, for the record shows that she received a renewed second grade teachers' certificate on July 1, 1922. A first grade certificate was issued July 1, 1926. She quite likely had some knowledge of French, for the connection with the nearby French island of St. Pierre,[3]

---

1. Men of a middle class between fish merchants and ordinary fishermen who would be supplied by the merchant to prosecute the fishery. They would then recruit fishermen to help in the conduct of the enterprise.
2. This is Lovell's inadvertent misspelling of Rompkey
3. St. Pierre and Miquelon are the only colonies in northern North America that remain part of France.

about twelve miles south of the Burin Peninsula, was quite strong. They were neighbours, perhaps somewhat more distant than other communities along the south coast, but nevertheless visited fairly frequently. As well, the residents of Belleoram, who numbered between 500 and 600 in the first decades of the century, came in contact with seamen of Spain and Portugal who brought home fish from Harvey and Company. So the sea was a highway that connected Belleoram to many parts of the world.

In Fanny's day, then, Belleoram would have been a largely homogeneous community where social activity, including the education system and community entertainment, revolved around the church. In times of emergency nearby communities were not within easy reach and the people had to rely on their own resources and to face the joys and calamities of life with courage and humour and equanimity. Dr. Conrad Fitzgerald[4] in St. Jacques told of the stoicism of the people, specifically how they endured pain in the days before anesthetics. A man with a large lymphoma (a fatty tumour) on his back decided to have it removed. He sat on a chair with his arms grasping the back, looking out the window with a

---

4. Conrad Fitzgerald of Marlboro, England, had worked as a ship's doctor travelling between London, India, and Australia. In 1873, at the request of a friend, he moved to Harbour Breton to work for Newman, Hunt and Company. Later he established his own medical practice in St. Jacques where he lived until his death in 1939. His practice took in the whole of Fortune Bay from Harbour Breton to Point Enragee, which he covered in a two-masted schooner of ten tons, usually alone except for his dog. His first boat, the *Albatross*, he sailed himself with a myriad of adventures. A man of skill, courage, and wit he became a legend on the coast.

view of the bay. As the doctor made a seven-inch incision over the tumour, the man remarked: "Doc, the wind is swinging from the north-northeast." Dr. Nigel Rusted in *It's Devil Deep Down There* remembers another story of stoicism. When Dr. Fitzgerald's son was home from medical school and wanting to do some surgery, the doctor let him remove a small cancer from a patient's lip. He took out a wedge without anesthetic; then asked his father if it was sufficient. Before the doctor could reply the patient interrupted with: "Make sure, doc. Take out another rasher."

In the early decades of the century Belleoram harbour would be full of fishing schooners. And as schooners needed sails there was a sail loft belonging to Harvey and Company where torn sails were mended by Reg Keeping and Harold Baker. On the upper storey was a large room with a huge sewing machine run by an engine on the lower level. Sometimes the men would have to work by lantern light to finish the sails for the schooners departing the next day.

In the lower level were the carpenters, my maternal grandfather, George Fudge, along with Frank Rose, Ernest Rose, Jerome Rose, as well as Lewis Cluett and Johnnie Rupert Cluett, the coopers. They built just about everything: dories, spars for schooners, whatever was needed. Off the carpenter shop was a forge where they made steel lunch buckets for the dorymen, two to a boat. Vernon Cluett's wife, Mary, the daughter of Reg Keeping, remembers fondly the warmth and cleanliness of the sail loft and the endless hours spent there, where a child could play and dream in comfort and safety.

The work ethic in Belleoram was strong. You worked to live. There were no movies; the people made their own entertainment. There would be school concerts including dialogues, songs, recitations and drills. Often there would be "times" in the Orange Hall which served as a community hall for country dances and square dances to the music of a violin or an accordion. Sometimes the church organ would be carried up to the Orange Hall to stand on an oak floor put there by my grandfather Fudge. There was often a music teacher in the community; in the 1920s and '30s this was Winnie Davidge, a predecessor in the music business of Bud Davidge of Simani. In the summer there was swimming down at the clear waters of the Barachois and in the winter skating on a pond in over the hill. After school boys and girls would haul their slides to the hill past John Cluett's old house and, warmly bundled, would careen down to the high road. Men built their own houses with a little help from family and friends. Sometimes a man would work late into the evening to get his house covered, his wife taking his supper to him so that he could carry on with his work.

Supplies came in bulk in the winter months: a barrel of apples or oranges would come from PEI or Nova Scotia, usually by a Harvey freighter, along with a case of loose tea, a case of Carnation milk, fresh pork, and potatoes. Similarly, household furnishings would be imported: mahogany dining sets, bedroom suites or armoires. Of course, you could shop at the Harvey store in Belleoram and buy a roast of frozen pork or beef or frozen vegetables to be kept outside in the cellar, for although there was no community electricity, Harvey's had their own generator. Or fresh meat, pork or herring might be kept in a barrel of brine. But there were real treats too; rum, raisins, figs, dried fruit, and other exotic foods. These treats would come back on Harvey ships like the *Sunset Glow* and the *Llewelyn* after dried fish was deposited in Spain or Portugal or Canada or the "Boston states." Alternatively, people might have goods and supplies come on the coastal boat from St. John's, shipped via Argentia, or they might come on the return vessel from Port aux Basques. Blueberries, raspberries and partridgeberries were to be had in abundance on outings that were a joyous part of community life. Some of these were made into jam and bottled. In the fall women would make pickles, some of rhubarb, others of cucumber and cauliflower. Some families kept chickens to supply them with fresh eggs or a meal for Sunday dinner. Harvey's would bring both soft and hard coal from Sydney and most houses had a grate in the dining room and in the living room and sometimes a stove at the foot of the stairs to send heat to the bedrooms. There was no running water so washing took place in the kitchen with water heated on the big stove. There were no hotels but some, like my grandmother Fudge and Mrs. Sceans, took in boarders. Dick Steele would come selling his crockery ware; Edgar Miller would come for Bowrings; W. H. Davidson, an English firm, was represented by a Mr. Dunn; George Evans would travel for Smallwood's Shoes. Often in the summer there were travelling students earning money for their education. Dr. Harry Roberts was one of these who appeared one summer selling magazines. As well there was a travelling dentist. Of course there was a resident doctor in the community operating a private practice out of his house while receiving a yearly stipend from the Government.

Before she went overseas Fanny was a teacher in a four-room school that taught kindergarten to grade eleven. Each of the four rooms had one teacher for about twenty students. Each student had his or her own desk with pencils and erasers and an inkwell for the nibs of their pens. There were lined exercise books and copy books where they learned to write, for penmanship was highly valued in the Newfoundland curriculum and remained so into the 1940s and '50s. And of course, the Royal Readers held a place of prominence.

FANNY AND VAD

This was the community from which the thirty-three-year-old Frances Cluett embarked on the coastal boat in 1916. She sailed out of Belleoram harbour and along the coast to Placentia, thence to St. John's, a trip she had made before. But this time surely the trip must have been made with excitement, anticipation and perhaps some apprehension, for this time she was off to join the VAD.

The Voluntary Aid Detachment had been formed in 1909 by the Red Cross and the Order of St. John of Jerusalem. Many women heard the call of King and Country in 1914 and were keen to contribute to the war effort. Some became nurses after doing a short course to obtain a certificate. Thereafter they worked side by side with regularly qualified nurses, assisting in hospitals at home and in all the major theatres of war. VADs also became fundraisers, cooks, kitchen maids, clerks, and ambulance drivers. Lady Davidson, the wife of the Governor, was heavily involved with the formation of VAD in Newfoundland and Labrador. It was she who formed The Patriotic Association of the Women of Newfoundland at the end of August 1914. It far outstripped its male counterpart in both organization and popular appeal. Organized principally by the wives of outport clergy, in little over a year it claimed 183 branches and had already enrolled 7,000 members from every walk of life to provide support for the war effort.

About 175 Newfoundland women served overseas as graduate nurses or with VAD, often close to the front lines. John Gallishaw in *Trenching in Gallipoli* recounts how:

> "Sisters of the VAD – Voluntary Aid Detachment – came in each afternoon to relieve the regular nursing sisters. They were mostly Englishwomen resident in Egypt. Most of their men folks were at one of the Fronts. They read to the men who could not hold books in their hands, talked to us cheerfully, and wrote letters for us. Some of them brought us little delicacies: grapes and chocolate. Men in hospital have no money. Any money they have is taken away when they arrive and refunded when they leave."[5]

Gallishaw is writing from Egypt but there were similar hospitals in France where Newfoundlanders had been

---

5. John Gallishaw, *Trenching in Gallipoli*, (Toronto: S.B Gundy, 1916), p. 123.

patients, fifteen of them in and around Rouen, Abbeville, Boulogne, and Etaples. Sir Edward Morris, when he visited, was gratified to find in the hospital in Etaples a large Newfoundland Ward with inscriptions over the beds indicating that they had been donated by school-children in Newfoundland. Before coming to France, the Prime Minister had spent an afternoon at the Wandsworth Hospital where he had seen 300 Newfoundland soldiers under treatment.

VAD, of course, was just a part of a much wider war effort by the old Dominion. Fanny was a Newfoundlander, one of the Island people whose lives and livelihood have been shaped by the sea. In 1914 Newfoundland was a self-governing dominion like Canada. Although it had rejected confederation with Canada in 1869, it was nevertheless heavily influenced by its western neighbour. Yet there was by this time a strong sense of identity in the old colony. Its people were not Canadians. They were Newfoundlanders with a distinctive culture shaped by their British and Irish traditions.

They were a religious people whose abiding faith carried them through tough times. In the city and in the outports, churches dominated the skyline. Religion shaped the dominion, exercising a strong influence on political life, controlling education and even functioning as a form of local government.

On the eve of the War, Newfoundland had a population of almost 250,000, 32,000 of whom lived in St. John's. The rest were scattered throughout 1,300 small communities around the rugged coastline. Its revenues were a modest $3.6 million annually while its public debt amounted to $30.5 million. Underpinned by the fishery, itself highly volatile and subject to both environmental vicissitudes and international politics and trade, the Dominion was hardly in a position to finance and maintain a standing regiment. Yet it did, even though it suffered mightily for it in later years.

For the first three years of the War the Newfoundland Government, knowing that it must remove party politics from the War, turned over the war effort to a group of private citizens, the Newfoundland Patriotic Association, led, albeit, by the Governor, Sir Walter Davidson. After this organization had equipped, transported, and cared for the Newfoundland land contingents, it was replaced by a Department of Militia. Over four years, more than 6,000 Newfoundland and Labrador men served in the Newfoundland Regiment, the Newfoundland Forestry Corps, the Canadian Expeditionary Force, and in other British Forces.

This is the milieu Fanny entered when she arrived in St. John's. How was she chosen? Why did she go? Did she hear the call of duty? Was it a question of service? What connections led her to join the VAD? We know that Harvey and Company in Belleoram where R. G. Pike was the manager had its head office in St. John's. And the Outerbridges and others in the firm had strong connections with the War and the military. Sir Joseph Outerbridge a principal shareholder and director of Harvey and Company, one of St. John's oldest and most important Water Street firms, was vice-chairman of the Newfoundland Patriotic Association. Lt. Norman A. Outerbridge, was killed near Monchy, while his brother, 2nd Lt. Herbert Outerbridge was seriously wounded at Sailly-Saillisel. Perhaps the connection came through the company. Or there may have been a church connection. The various brigades that were largely church-based formed the bulk of the first 500. Perhaps Fanny's connection was through the church. We know that Rev. Jacob Brinton,[6] a prominent church son of Belleoram, was a prime contact for her after she arrived in St. John's and helped her to deal with officialdom. Both she and her cousin, Vince Cluett, used his presence and position in preparing themselves for overseas. Then again, Vince had decided to volunteer, as had others from Belleoram, and perhaps their patriotism and their call to service and adventure spurred Fanny's own commitment. Or it may be that the call for her came from the Women's Patriotic Association. Before she volunteered she had been Belleoram President of the Women's Patriotic Association, supervising the knitting that went into the kits going to the servicemen overseas. And when the soldiers came home on leave she made sure they were given a warm welcome with a special tea and a talk to the ladies about their experiences. Fittingly, when she herself came home from the War there was a welcome arch constructed near her house in Belleoram and she was presented with a bouquet of flowers by Lavina (Fudge) Hardiman.

Whatever the motivation or circumstances of her joining VAD she was no stranger to leadership and service. Her father died when she was still young and obviously she assumed a mantle of leadership within the family. And this

---

6. The son of Charlie Brinton and Susannah Rompkey he was trained at Durham, England, from which university he later received an honorary Master of Arts.

mantle of leadership extended to the community for she was clearly a leader in church and state. In addition to her role as teacher, she was President of the Attar Guild and looked after the altar with great care and reverence. Until her death in 1969 there were always fresh flowers from her garden on the altar. But she was also called upon for medical help, even though she had no training until she went to St. John's. She was an attractive woman, mature, intelligent, efficient, physically fit, a team player. Fanny was a woman of spirit, one part courage, and one part humour.

Although initially astonished by the comparative affluence and grandeur of the St. John's elite, she was by no means intimidated by it and immediately adapted to her circumstances with equanimity. She found her equipment and kit and took her training with aplomb. Some of her companions, including John Gallishaw's sister, Henrietta, became lifelong friends. With traces of Old World courtesy, Fanny will often refer to her friend with whom she rooms as "Miss Gallishaw" while at other times it is just "Gallishaw," the use of the last name only being the usual form of address between nurses. Then the trips to New York and later to Liverpool and Lincoln, where she completed her training, brought more new experiences, the joy and astonishment of which she shared with her mother in great detail. Cluett was chosen early to go to France ahead of those who had preceded her to London and she was also singled out for special duty in the field where hospitals were closer to the battlefield and where, therefore, the casualties and the wounds would have been more severe, requiring swift and sure treatment. She was transferred to Istanbul in 1919 after some of her fellow VADs had been demobbed. Did she volunteer to go to Istanbul or was she asked? Fanny was a leader and no doubt her superiors recognized that leadership. But it is also clear that Fanny was prepared from the beginning to give the last full measure of service.

THE CLUETT LETTERS

Her letters show Fanny Cluett to be a woman of self-confidence, courage, determination, humour, intelligence, strong faith, devotion to service, and a woman with a strong Newfoundland identity. They paint the War from the perspective of the nurse, of one who saw the casualties, of one who experienced the horror, of one who saw the pain and the sacrifice, the ultimate service.

She was thrust into previously unknown climes and circumstances and showed that she could handle these with strength and dignity. There, in environments that were new to her and that were seized by the turmoil and terror of war, she took it all in her stride. In the hospitals and on the wards she experienced and dealt with the worst the War had to offer: the most painful illnesses, suicide, and death. Once, on a free day, alone in France she was knocked down by a horse. Even though those around her knew little or no English, she used her common sense and her meagre knowledge of French to extract herself from a difficult situation. She had to work with new mates and new superiors in tasks for which she had perhaps a minimal amount of training. But she learned quickly. She made friends easily and kept them, as her letters show. Once, during a storm, it was to Fanny's bed that a terrified fellow nurse turned. All of this she handled with courage and competence all the while maintaining a healthy sense of humour; on an outing in France she is amused by two lovers who carry on a silly courtship in what to her was a foreign language.

Cluett's letters are her immediate reactions, often in an idiom that Belleoramers would appreciate. They include as well as medical observations, descriptions of clothes and styles and the simple *joie de vivre* that men and women find in each other's company.

Why did she write them? Naturally she wanted a record of a unique experience, but the letters provided, as well, a therapy with which to treat the horrors of war. They are her tie with home; they are her lifeline. No matter where she goes or what she does she is a Cluett from Belleoram. That is her touchstone. That is her grounding. With its trace of Old World charm one of Fanny's favourite expressions is "my word!" Indeed, her word is her bond and her bond is her word. The words she sends to her mother and her friends are simply a continuation of the chatter around the kitchen table or at the Altar Guild, the verbal chain that holds together this closely knit society. It is a society where there is a great deal of mutual respect, particularly for elders and children. Mother is "Mother" and father is "Father" and there are many "uncles" and "aunts." There is mutual dependency, mutual respect, and mutual affection. She does share some of horrors of the war but spares her family from the full brunt of it:

"Many a bedside have I stood by and watched the last breath, with the rats rushing underneath the bed . . ." she wrote from Rouen.

"This is a very wicked world . . . you cannot realize what sufferings there are. Some of the misery will ever live in my memory. It seems to me now as though I shall always have sad thoughts in my eyes."

She describes the illnesses and the cures in great detail. As well she has the eye of the novelist for the detail of life, the dress, the foods, the joy and wonder at different types of weather. Some of her accounts, such as those of the patient Rosee, are amusing, revealing and fetching.

Her social life revolves around her fellow VADs. They choose to attend services and parades and concerts, to go for walks, to see the sights of France and England. She clearly makes fast friends and many of her fellows clearly look to her for comfort and companionship. She enjoys her social life with the VADs just as she enjoyed the times and the concerts in Belleoram.

Through it all she is faithful to her roots, faithful to her family and her home. There must have been a special relationship with her mother, whom she writes regularly and most often. But all of the Cluetts are special for her and she hunts them down wherever she can. Her inability to find her cousin, Vince, before he dies is especially poignant. She never forgets Belleoram, which has formed her. And she is not a Canadian but a Newfoundlander whose identity is strong and distinct just as was that of the soldiers of the Newfoundland Regiment who scorned recognition as Canadians, as was so often wont to happen.

She may have been bruised but she was not broken by

the War. Afterwards she returned to teaching in Belleoram. Her students, particularly Leah Taylor and Dorothy (Kearley) Petite, remember her as a wonderful teacher, strict but with a wealth of experience who made sure they heard about history and the stories of heroes. She read to them each day with "such expression and feeling," and taught them the finer points of needlework. She shared with them her experiences of the customs, places and people she had met. To them she was a heroine, one who would from time to time bring souvenirs, such as her gas mask, to the school to remind them of her time at the Front.

She was strict. Once when Bert May was chasing Leah Taylor in school the race down the corridor resulted in the demolition of the pencil sharpener. Fanny was angry and the culprits received a scolding. They apologized, of course, but although accepted it was not enough. "That won't mend it," Fanny scolded. The pencil sharpener had to be replaced.

But outside school there was always a twinkle in her eye as she continued to serve young and old alike. She was in constant demand as a nurse. "We soon won't have a sheet left in the house," her mother observed, "Fan will have them all torn up for bandages."

She was a very special woman who left a very special account of her wartime experiences. Fanny's letters speak for themselves. They are published here as she wrote them with only a minimum of editing.

Bill Rompkey
July 2006

THE LETTERS

Belleoram
May 3rd 1908

Dear Lil,[1]

I have so much to tell you, I hardly know when & how to begin. You see I have started writing in an exercise, expecting to write it through: but I daresay before I get half way through it, I shall be tired. We received your post cards & were more than glad to hear from you, as you have not written so long, owing to the Bruce's[2] being stopped in the ice I suppose.

Granfer[3] came down next day, so I gave him the post card you sent. He was delighted. He says "Winnie still knows I am in the land of the living." (He calls you Winnie). Then he asks me what it would cost to put a stamp on an envelope. I told him two cents. He then wanted to know where they were to be got. I told him, at the post office. He went off with that much. I thought he was going to write you.

By & by, mother[4] came in with two cents Granfer had

1. Her sister, Lillian Cluett (1880–1938), then in Sydney, Nova Scotia.
2. Newfoundland Railway coastal boat.
3. Her uncle, Levi Cluett, the son of John and Sarah (Tulk) Cluett. Levi married Martha Rompkey: their children were Winifred, Henrietta Bishop Cluett, known as "Bish"—blind for much of her life, Susanna who married Captain Johnnie Brinton, and William.
4. Matilda Grandy Cluett (1855–1931), a daughter of John and Maria Grandy.

given her for me. I was obliged to laugh. I don't know what I have to do with them. I suppose I must buy a post card and put his name on it. Isn't it funny! Look out next time for this famous post card from Granfer. I shall have to pay my own two cents to send it. If I had known at first that it was to buy a post card, I might have asked him for 4 cents; but you know I thought he was going to write a letter, and wanted a two-cent stamp. Poor Granfer, he is laughable some times.

Isn't it a lovely day to day. Just a little wind; but so fine. Mother is gone to prayers[5] & I am alone writing this. Win[6] is just gone down. Joseph[7] has been in all this morning. I looked out the window and saw Julie leading him up through. He looked so pretty. He had on a blue velvet tam[8] and a blue velvet dress trimmed with narrow white braid. I knocked to the window for him to come in. As soon as he came in he wanted a tick (stick)[9] for Annie (He calls me Annie). He came in the other day while I was out, and looked under the table for Annie. He always wants this "tick." It came about this way. One evening I was cleaning out the long cubboard [sic], & with the old rubbish I had taken out was a stick. Joseph came in the midst of it, got the stick and began running after me everywhere. He enjoyed it so much. Ever since then he wants a stick when he comes in.

5. Rev. MacDermott has pointed out that people go to prayers, not to service. Service is something you give; prayers are something you attend or practice.
6. Winifred, daughter of Levi Cluett, married Sam Joe Burdock.
7. A young cousin, the son of Winifred and Sam Joe Burdock.
8. A flat, round, brimless cap like a beret; the name comes from tam-o'-shanter.
9. Perhaps a walking stick or cane, very fashionable especially with the older men.

After that I began cleaning out the chest. Naturally he wanted to get in. I said to him, "Fannie doesn't like Dodo". (He calls himself Dodo.) He came along and puts up his sweet little face for me to kiss him; but he is a terror when he gets vexed. He says "bugger" now. Win will have something to do to mind him this summer. You should see him blowing bubbles. He is a very pretty child, so tiny. I was going to take him to Sunday school to day, had there been any Children Service. He followed us up through the path last Sunday, and tumbled down in the midst of the mud and everything. He wouldn't let Win clean him. Mother had to do it. He is simply ruined; but Win says he is afraid of the stick, she has only to show it to him.

Tell Bish[10] we are going to have a Guild[11] Sociable to morrow night in the Guild Room. We joined Lizzy Holmans & Miss Grouchy[12] last meeting. We balloted for them the meeting before and they were elected, so we initiated them last meeting. I only wish you had been there. What stamping & clapping when they are elected; but so dismal when they are black balled.

To this Sociable we are going to ask the old men of Belleoram, whom we think had not much enjoyment Xmas. The choir boys are also opening with us. There

10. Henrietta Bishop Cluett, a cousin, the daughter of Uncle Levi Cluett, her father's brother.
11. The Altar Guild of the Anglican Church had its own building near the rectory. The activities were not necessarily confined to support and care for the altar and the chancel.
12. Rev. Grouchy was the Anglican minister at Belleoram 1907 to 1909; the reference is to his daughter.

will be such a crowd, we won't have room enough to turn round.

The other night after joining those two, we had games until ten o'clock. It was just grand.

Little Ida has a mind to join; but she can't come to the point of joining. I just love to be balloting for them. My nerves are strung to their utmost, as we can't tell whether they are elected or not until everyone has finished her portion of work required for the occasion.

—

Saturday night [May 9]

We scrubbed the Guild Room today, such a crowd of us. The Women's Association[13] work in the same room. They bought the stove and lamps and curtains for the room. We bought six bolts of paper to paper it. We are now going to order for a large frosted glass for the door, which will cost us $4.00 or thereabouts. It is rather expensive isn't it. I don't know why there was such a large place left for a glass. Of course we can get an ordinary glass much cheaper than $4.00; but Mr. Grouchy wishes to have one opaque, so that we won't see in his rooms, and they won't see in our room. We are also going to buy white paint for the doors and windows. We shall start painting it the coming week. Mr. Grouchy suggested that we should get oil cloth for the floor; but we are not all in favour of it; as there are two societies using it; but we

---

13. The Church of England Women's Association (CEWA), a support group of the Anglican Church.

may change our minds later on, as we are all working or aiming at the one object.

I wish you could see the organ, it is just grand; but it is in debt a little yet. We have paint to paint the inside of the Church.

When Edward Owen Fudge[14] & Manuel Poole came from Oporto[15] a short while ago they brought some artificial flowers & presented them to the Church. Very good of them, wasn't it. They are placed on the altar.

I am going to make an ensign for the Guild with G.S.P.B. on it: that is, the Guild of St. Perpetua; so that whenever we want to call a meeting, simply hoist the flag.

I only wish you could see mother to night. She is framing pictures. One of the frames is that famous drawing slate frame, and two others are mirror frames. One of which I broke over to the Candy Party last winter and the other one you & I — I suppose — broke in the old house (ha! ha!), I wish you could also see our kitchen table, the uproar it is in. I am writing, so of course there is this book on it, and a bottle of ink and mother framing pictures, and a hammer and scissors, and a photograph & a work box and a piece of art muslin and the machine and two lamps, and a piece of

---

14. Captain Edward Owen Fudge, the son of Silas and a brother of John Marshall Fudge, left school at the age of twelve and not long after went to sea, eventually rising to command fishing vessels. He was noted for his high-line fishing and his unique ability as a sea captain. He established a record in St. John's for the fastest trip to Oporto by a sailing vessel. During WWII he was a Flying Officer with the RCAF Marine Division.

15. Vessels would take a cargo of dried cod to Oporto, Portugal, and return with a load of salt for curing the fish.

shingle, and the dining room drapery, & the corner drapery and stockings, I bet you never saw anything equal to it. Mother will certainly kill herself working at this picture framing business. It would make a cat laugh to watch her, & she is scrunching something so much, it goes right through my whole system.

(I got to get something to eat before I write any more; but how can I write with mother hammering on the table; but I think she is making a poor hand at framing.) I don't think mother will ever tire of talking about St. John's. We get into some yarns sometimes about it. I suppose it seemed awfully strange to her; but Lil she would just love to go again.

Mrs. Brinton[16] went on the Glencoe[17] to St John's, Thursday, where she will reside for the future. She had a message from Jake saying he was not very well so off she started; but she intended going later on. Critchel has her place, the house, etc.

When I was to St John's last fall, I bought a winter's coat $7.50, dark fawn, or exactly the shade of that one Sam Joe[18] brought me from Sydney. It hangs loose at the back with stitchings. A very heavy coat. I also had a wine coloured skirt and white silk for a blouse. I have the blouse nearly worn out. It was made with six or seven rows of shirring for a yolk and two thin narrow tucks just

16. The mother of Rev. Jacob Brinton, parish priest at the Anglican Cathedral in St. John's for over forty years, and a chief point of contact for the Belleoram diaspora.
17. MV *Glencoe*, a Newfoundland Railway coastal boat carrying passengers, freight and mail along the coast.
18. Burdock.

above the waist & a box plait of wide insertion from the yolk to the waist.

Mother has a very nice bonnet, coronet shaped. It is more like a hat than a bonnet, very pretty. You know my raglan, mother wasted a can of paint over it, I really can't wear [it] anymore, especially on Sundays; but says for me to cut it off for her. I ordered for another last week. Violet did me a hat this winter. You know that green plush one of mine, well I ripped it up & sent the plush to Violet to do me another which she did. It was made sailor shape with beautiful ribbon loops on each side of the crown and two quills and a lift under the crown of dark green silk. I was charmed with it. Reta told me it was the best thing I ever put on my head. I also have a black velvet one with black silk ribbon across the crown & tied in a knot and big black feathers hanging over the side. It wasn't very expensive. We are not quite finished house cleaning yet. We have some pieces of canvas to paint. We painted the dining room doors and windows white & the floor cherry red. It is papered dark green with white bordering of roses & leaves nearly 16 inches wide, perhaps wider.

I painted the floor of the hall cherry red and am going to do the stair banisters and post a shade of green like I saw on Johnny Lee's boat. We are going to paint the floor of the kitchen yellow. We did nothing to the parlour or the dining room ceiling as we are thinking of getting it done with hard wood.

I have some oil cloth for my room. I think it is very pretty. Mother had a set of lace curtains for Art's[19] room.

---

19. Fanny's brother Arthur (1888–1963).

I have hooked no mat this year. I brought one down from Burgeo last summer to hook for Julia Matthews & haven't touched it yet. We are always so busy at something another. Our Guild meeting on Wednesday night & then the Sociable on Monday night and prayers Friday night. Sometimes we call two meetings a week; when Mr. Grouchy wishes to propose something.

This week I am going to clean the flower garden. I had some pansies and Nasturtiums and Shirley Poppies from Toronto. I also ordered for peonies & rose trees but did not get them as the duty to send them was 30 cents; but I must send right on and get them. I think our rose trees are going to be good this year.

(Mother is hard at framing yet. She just said, "tis so warm" and no wonder, its hammering and fixing pictures, no stop at all).

I must now tell you about the two concerts, viz—: Women's[20] & ours[21]. Some people said the women's was best, perhaps it was but we made most money, realizing $35.50. After our concert the women sold refreshments, making $6.00.

We have had a picture taken of the way we were dressed in one part of the concert. I shall send it to you for inspection as soon as I get it; but you must return it again. Mr. Staples took it. He is a first rate hand at it.

We opened our concert with "Jingle Bells," keeping time by marching; then it was "Scene in a Backwood School," then "Topsy Turvy" then "Skidmore Guards"

20. The CEWA, Church of England Women's Association.
21. The Guild of St. Perpetua.

— that was very nice —. Reat and Rhynie[22] and Tryphie[23] sang "When the leaves came drifting down." Ida[24] and Miss Grouchy & I sang "Three old maids at Lee." I wish you could have seen our bonnets. Miss Grouchy and I trimmed them one night down to our place. Frances played to our concert and Ida to the Association. They opened theirs with "Red, White & Blue" waving their ribbons back and forth. This song Mrs. Grouchy composed. It was good, being all about the organ etc, just lovely. "Whispering Hope" was sung by Julie Burdock, Martha Keeping, Aunt Christian. Ernest John[25] and Mrs. Grouchy joining in the chorus. It sounded very nice. Ernest John and Mrs. Grouchy acted "Tit for Tit." It wasn't bad at all. Levi Angus[26] and Julie Pine[27] and Mrs. Pearce acted one. I can't tell you about it as it will take me all night and take all my paper too: Emily Jane Dicks and Stella acted "Counting Eggs." It was splendid, the best of all I think. Emily Jane did her part exceedingly well. First when she began I could not tell who it was. She pronounced her words just as they ought. I loved that piece, it was rather comical. Levi

---

22. Perhaps Rhyna (Cluett) Taylor, although Vincent Taylor says it was also a nickname for Maria Grandy Cluett, a cousin, sister to Ray and Vincent Cluett.
23. Tryphina Fudge.
24. Ida Cluett.
25. Burdock.
26. Levi Angus McCuish, her neighbour who was the Customs Officer in Belleoram and whose daughter, Flora, married Captain Gabriel Fudge, one of the local fishing skippers who later became captain of the *Malakoff* and the *Arctica* in the bait service of the Province.
27. Daughter of Ben Pine, a Fortune Bay skipper, who was the owner of the American vessel *Arthur D Storey*.

Angus and Mrs. Grouchy sang "Gathering up the shells from the shore". Their voices blended together very nicely indeed. English Harbour[28] R.C. Teacher & Effie Evans and Lil Evans and Rich Marshall were down, also the Burke boys.[29] (I must put this up now, and prepare for bed, it is half past eleven and mother hammering still.)

—

Sunday Afternoon [May 10]

We just finished dinner, mother and I, and before I get ready for school,[30] I shall write a little more. I really believe it is going to rain, and it was so beautiful just now.

Nina Yarns baby died a short while ago: she had something wrong with her brain, poor child, I don't know what caused it. Simeon[31] has been dreadfully sick. He had a sore throat, so sore, that when he received Holy Communion by Mr. Grouchy it ran out through his nose. It's a miracle he didn't choke. The doctor ordered him to paint[32] it, which he did. Just fancy one having to paint his throat.

---

28. A community about nine miles west of Belleoram along the coast.
29. Evans and Burke are well-known names in St. Jacques, the closest community to Belleoram which shared its participation in the bank fishery. It had a great harbour and a wonderful beach for drying fish. The Burkes operated the largest business in the community.
30. Sunday school where Fanny taught.
31. Simeon Cluett.
32. Painting the affected part was done with iodine, the cure-all in those days.

Ida told me, her mother called her one morning to go up in the room to see her father. She looked through the door & he was sleeping or they thought he was, with his eyes half open. They thought it was all over with him. He would have died only he was treated so well.

Ida said she thought that if he had died, they would be left the same as we were.[33] He would wake up in the nights & have to drink vinegar straight away to clear his throat. The doctor said it was an uncommon sore throat; but I should say it was next to diphtheria, however it has taken all the flesh off him & left him a mere skeleton. Poor man, nobody knows only himself what he has gone through; but we can imagine how he must have suffered when we looked at him. He is able to come downstairs now. In the morning he was to St. Jacques as smart as could be. In the evening he was taken like this, very suddenly.

Win has just brought in Joseph; but mother and he are gone out again.

I must put this up again and start getting ready for school, as it is just 2 o'clock by our time, and Children's Service is at 3 o'clock; but School[34] between. We have our school painted tip top now. The sides of the interior are painted pea green with dark red trimmings. The wide trimmings you know on the side, that was varnished before are now painted dark red. The windows white. The cupboards green panels with white facings. The porches are done to

---

33. Fanny's father, Arthur Cluett (1851–1897), died when she was only fourteen.
34. Meaning Sunday School.

match the body. It seemed so strange at first, that I really thought it must be another school.

Mr. Chant[35] is getting the Mission House[36] white washed with Cherry Red facings. It doesn't look a bit like the same house. They are painting it inside too and canvassing it.

You say you would change sausages for cabbage. I wish I were near you. We haven't had any sausages since Art left the last time. We have some cabbage left from last year. We are talking of having cabbage cooked over in the Guild Room later on. I prefer sausages — twenty times over — to cabbage. I am positively certain I should never tire of sausages, they are scrumptious.

I suppose you know Will is sick, (Uncle Levi's Will) I have just been in too see him: but he says he is a little better to day. Mr. Grouchy was down to see him the other day. He has been miserable enough. He strained his side while working at something another[37] and the result has been very bad indeed. He was sick for a time & got out: now he hasn't been able to get out this long time. Isn't he thin, his cheekbones are so high. Mr. Grouchy told me that Uncle Levi was nervous, I suppose he thought that Will was very miserable; but he is over the dangerous point the Dr. said. Mother says he is a little better too.

Watson[38] hasn't done anything this year, owing to

---

35. School principal in Belleoram at the time.
36. Teachers' residence.
37. A typical local expression that seems to have been used for "something or other."
38. Watson Cluett.

the rheumatism which he has about him. When Will got out, there used to be the three of them, Watson and Will and Will Fudge walking about. Neither of them able to do anything. Will Fudge has consumption in his left arm. He keeps a shingle on it all the time. The Dr. healed his lungs & now it has shown itself in his arm; but he looks so well, his face so red and healthy looking, however his looks deceive him.

After Children's Service to day Sal[39] & I went right around to the point of beach & then on board of "The Gay Gordon."[40] She is a splendid vessel. It is the one that Edward Owen[41] and Will John Rose and Albert Willie and Manuel Poole went across to Oporto in. A man took us down the cabin. She is very nicely done & looks so large.

Tell Bish we have had our Guild Sociable: but not half the girls went. My partner was Uncle Levi, Rhynie had Uncle John (Watson's father). Stel[42] had Mr. Isaac Burke[43] who is down here repairing his boat. Reta had Phillip Cluett. Beat Kearley had Mr. Pearce and Hilda[44] Tom Drakes. Frances[45] had her Grandfather, and Mr. Grouchy was out with us. We had a gay time. I think the old fellows enjoyed themselves immensely. Mr. Pearce

39. Sally Kearley.
40. A tern schooner belonging to Kearleys used to carry dried codfish overseas. Other Kearley vessels had romantic names like the *Sparkling Glance*.
41. Edward Owen Fudge.
42. Stella Kearley.
43. From St. Jacques.
44. Hilda Kearley.
45. Frances McCuish.

danced so many times. Uncle Levi sat back and killed himself laughing at them. Just imagine Phillip Cluett and Mr. Pearce and Uncle Jo[h]nie and them dancing. I shall never forget it. Rhynie laughed so much out in the first dance that she had to sit.

We had games of all kinds. I wish you had been there when we were redeeming the forfeits.[46] Tryphie and Mr. Pearce had to dance a step dance on the table; and they did it too. Mr. Burke played for them on his violin which he brought especially for the occasion. He can play splendidly; we owe him thanks for being so kind as to bring his violin & play so often for us.

There was one game we had, I forget now what it is called; but all the ladies are on one side of the room and the gents on the other side. I headed the girls and Mr. Grouchy the men. Whatever he would say to the men to do, they had to do it. Of course he would do it first to show. Then I would do the same thing on my side, right down through the whole crowd. By and By, when we got them as far as to kneel on the floor on one knee in single file, we gave then a push. Off goes the whole lot of them on the floor in a heap. That's when we had it. I shall never forget when I looked over at the men, to see nothing but whiskers and grey heads all around the stove. I wonder they didn't push it down while falling, however they didn't.

I think it's only right and proper for us to get up something to make the older folks enjoy themselves. I am afraid I won't finish this now before the steamer comes, as she is

---

46. "Redeeming the Forfeits"; the player had to do whatever was on a slip of paper picked from a bag by the team leader.

expected shortly; and must get ready for prayers. Mother is getting ready.

What is the style of summer hats at Sydney this year? Ida and Sally and I are going to get one. Ida & Ida were talking at first of having a flop hat; but I think I shall have another kind now. Are they worn large or small? Of course I can send for the latest style.

Miss Grouchy wore a very pretty one this morning. It was open straw trimmed with roses and blue ribbon. Her favorite colour is blue. She has some very pretty dresses, among them, she wears a blue one. I admired it very much: so she tells me she will have her picture taken for one when she goes home, and will wear that dress. We are great chums. I have been over to the Parsonage with her often. She is one who doesn't mind in the least what you say to her. She has been spending a time with Mrs. Fitzgerald.[47]

—

Sunday noon again [May 17]

I did not finish my letter to send it last Sunday: but will try now. Mother is just having her dinner, but I am going to wait until I finish this bit.

Watson & Lewis are just gone out. We have been playing and singing hymns. Watson is now able to work on the road; but feels his feet very tender from the rheumatism.

---

47. Wife of Dr. Conrad Fitzgerald, the doctor stationed in St. Jacques.

Will[48] is beginning to eat now, which is a sure sign that he is getting better.

One of Dick Marshall's brothers died a short while ago in consumption.

This is a beautiful day; but very windy. Mother was more than glad of the blouse you sent her. I had a pompadour down St. John's like the one you sent me so I put this one away for the future. It was a sweet little calendar you sent Art. Didn't you say you had a post card album for me? Violet sent me one that holds 180; I have quite a lot in it. I had six pictures of New York not long ago. I think Abe sent them to me, as he promised to send me some.

Is Ida coming this summer? Tell her to come on. We will go out rowing again and berry picking & nobody knows what. How was it she did not answer my letter. Wasn't it worth answering? We have our back kitchen floor painted; so to day we are living in the parlour.

Granfer came in and didn't know which way to go. I peeped out around the parlour[49] door, he was just opening the back room door. I must now get ready for school. Remember me to Bish & Ida and Aunt Sarah[50] etc.

Good Bye

from Fanny. Write soon.

---

48. Will Fudge.
49. The front room or living room.
50. Mrs. Walter Cluett, sister of Fanny's mother, Matilda.

Granfer just looked at that original flower pot you made
that time and asked if that wasn't what Winnie made.
He said you see all that kind of stuff; but suppose you
didn't have time to make it up there (ha! ha!).

Newfoundland Postal Telegraphs
1103 am
St. John's
2/10/16

To Miss Frances Cluett

Expect you this week.

Mrs. Browning[1]

---

1. Adeline Hubert (1869–1950) of Jersey in the Channel Islands married John Browning, a St. John's businessman in 1894. President of the Vigornia Branch of the Red Cross Association under the Women's Patriotic Association, she also chaired the Ladies Committee for the reception of returned soldiers and helped found the Jensen Camp for tuberculosis-ridden soldiers. She received the O.B.E. in March 1917. In 1918 she was promoted to C.B.E.

Dear Mother,

I arrived at St. John's Friday around 2 p.m. Wasn't a bit seasick coming, no more than on the land. We had good run right from Belleoram. Emily Pike[2] got on at St. Lawrence, so I had great company from that down. I haven't seen her since we landed.

At Placentia we had to go to Mrs. Dumfey's and get a cup of tea, as we had to leave the Glencoe[3] at 6 a.m: so I didn't feel like going on the train without something, we had to pay twenty cents. I just had a cup of tea and a bit

---

1. The King George V Seamen's Institute was founded in 1912 by Sir Wilfred Grenfell. Located on the east end of Water Street in downtown St. John's, the building was on property donated to the Royal National Mission to deep-sea-fishermen by Edgar Bowring. From 1914 until the Depression, it provided accommodations and entertainment to visiting seamen. There was a twenty-four-hour booking service: single and double rooms for twenty and thirty-five cents respectively, a restaurant, billiards, a pool, a bowling alley, a library with reading rooms and writing tables; as well, there were lectures and entertainment. The "Girls' Department" had a separate entrance and different rules for board and lodging. In World War II the building was reopened as the Caribou Hut to offer housing and entertainment to various military personnel passing through St. John's.
2. Sister to Neil Pike of St. John's, a member of the Newfoundland Regiment. Fanny and her family knew the Pikes.
3. Newfoundland Railway steamer serving the south coast.

of bread and butter. We left Placentia at 7.20 am and got in St. John's around 2 p.m.

Mrs. Browning, Lady Davidson's secretary[4] and Dr. Patterson's[5] wife were at the station to meet me. You can imagine what I felt like. They were dressed to kill, and I had on my flake boots[6] and old blue coat. Mrs. Browning had on a fawn suit and brown velvet hat and furs. She had previously arranged for me to room at the Institute; but it was filled then owing to the strike on the Portia. So Mrs. Browning invited me up at her house. It is in the same grounds with the Government House. We drove up there in a cab. Oh my! I only wish you could see the inside of that house. The first I did was had a wash in the bath room, then we had luncheon in the dining room, and five o'clock tea in the dining room and supper in the breakfast room. I wish you could have seen us sitting at the five o'clock tea table with so much silver ware. Before we started the maid pushed across the folding doors; before that it was all one. I can never tell you what it is like. The stairs are done with red plush, all winding, and five or six could walk up side by side. Miss McDwyer, a young girl came in the afternoon and helped us to pack barrels of bandages for the soldiers. We packed five barrels. Mrs. Browning would write the

---

4. Lady Davidson was the wife of the Governor of Newfoundland, Sir Walter Davidson, who was head of the Newfoundland Patriotic Association.
5. Dr. Lamont Paterson was a medical officer with the Newfoundland Regiment. Fanny inadvertently misspelled Paterson in her letter.
6. Rubber boots worn by women making fish on the flakes.

numbers on the rolls of bandages and I would stamp them.

By and by a telephone call came saying the Portia had gone therefore there was room for me at the Institute. At 8 p.m. Mrs. Browning took me down to British Hall[7] to the lecture room. I was just a little late. There were seven girls already there. Dr. Reeves[8] lectured to us, then we had to apply bandages ourselves. I got an introduction to a Miss Janes;[9] so I applied bandages on her. Mrs. Browning and the Dr. looking on. The first bandage went round the arm and body. Second fracture we had to splint the arm, and bandage also put in sling. Third bandage was around the elbow, fourth bandage around the fore arm, the last one around the hand.

Miss Janes is going to call for me at 3 p.m. this evening. We are going to practice bandaging again.

---

7. A three-storey brick building on the southwest corner of the intersection of Bond and Flavin streets. It was the second hall of the British Society, founded in 1832 by "staunch male Protestants devoted to king and country." It was purchased by the Church of England in 1918 and converted into Bishop Spencer College.

8. Likely she refers to Lieutenant William Reeves, a member of the Church Lads Brigade, one of the first groups to sign up for St. John Ambulance training. In 1912 the C.L.B. trainees were formed into Ambulance Division No. 1. When the War broke out, the chief medical officer of the Newfoundland Regiment, Dr. Cluny MacPherson, formed the first Medical Battalion entirely out of No.1 members. Most of the battalion were stretcher bearers and medics on the front lines, but some stayed behind to help the Standing Medical Board in Newfoundland check volunteers, maintain barracks hygiene, and help with returned disabled soldiers. Lt. Reeves helped Major Paterson in barracks work in St. John's. He was well qualified to teach advanced first aid.

9. A fellow VAD, Clare Janes and Frances Cluett would become fast friends.

Monday night at 8 p.m. another lecture. Tuesday at 3 p.m. we have to go to Mrs. Browning's to help her again to pack.

Just a minute ago, Mrs. Davidson matron of this Institute, came in to say that Mrs. Browning had called in the morning to say that arrangements were already made as regards my board etc, and that I had nothing at all to bother about. You need not say that to anyone else, as I cannot say if the other girls are so well looked after; so I wouldn't want it to be known.

We are rushed with training, and will I am afraid be sent across quicker than I thought. Of course I can't say for sure: but Mrs. Browning told me last night that perhaps we would be through in five weeks.

St. John's has to be in darkness, hardly any lights on the automobiles or street cars. The girls at the Institute turned out the lights in the music room. St. John's is being guarded.[10]

I had to get a waist this morning to wear at Mrs. Browning's on Tuesday. Her house is like a palace, the conservatory is splendid, you can hardly find your way around.

Tell Leah[11] I am sleeping in the bed she left; but am going to be changed in another room to-night.

---

10. St. John's was darkened in the fall of 1916 and again, under the auspices of the War Measures Act, in the summer of 1917. As of October 1916, St. John's harbour was closed at night until further notice (a boom was laid across the Narrows) and city lights completely muffled until daybreak to protect against possible German attacks. As well, the Cape Spear lighthouse was dimmed, the harbour leading lights, and Fort Amherst lights were extinguished and all vehicle lights were also to be dimmed to twenty-five per cent of their usual glare.
11. Drake, later Leah Dicks.

I am enclosing a note for Rhynie. Judge Johnson's[12] two daughters are studying Red Cross too.

I might have seen Leah before she left as I was at the Institute before she left to go abroad.

Good Bye Mother.
Don't worry about me.
From your daughter Fanny.

---

12. Born in St. John's, George Macness Johnson studied law in England and returned to be the sole partner of Sir William Whiteway's law firm. Johnson maintained the law firm while Whiteway pursued his political career. He was named an Associate Judge of the Supreme Court of Newfoundland in 1902. His daughters, Sybil and Estelle were VADs.

Seamen's Institute
St. John's
NFLD
Oct. 29/16

Sunday

Dear Mother,

This is certainly a beautiful day. I went to Holy Communion this morning at 8 a.m. with Miss Tizzard a girl who is boarding here. We went to the Cathedral. Mr. Brinton administered Holy Communion.

Last night Vince[1] called for me, we went to Mr. Brinton's to get a recommendation. I have to get two before I can leave St. John's. I should have got them before I left home: however it does not matter, as Vince phoned Mr. Thompson, and he wrote one for me, so I have the two of them now. Miss Janes and I went to Dr. Burden's last Tuesday night to be examined on First Aid and Home Nursing. The both of us passed. He asked us quite a few questions. Miss Janes was supposed to have a broken collar bone and a severe bleeding from the palm of the hand which could not be stopped, I of course had to treat it. He

---

1. A cousin, the son of Walter and Sarah Cluett, Vince Cluett was an officer in the Newfoundland Regiment and a brother to Rhynie and Ray. He was one of the officers who, with 100 men, embarked from Halifax on April 18, 1916 on the *Northland*. They were en route to Ayr to reinforce the Regiment. He died of his wounds at St. John's Hospital, Etaples, following the fighting at Masnières in November 1917.

then asked me how I would change an under sheet for a person who was very ill. He then asked me what I would do in a case of diphtheria, what disinfectants I would use, and how strong to use them. I had to read the clinical thermometer, and treat a case of poisoning. He asked me how to make a linseed meal poultice, etc. He asked a good many questions.

After he told us we had passed you can imagine how light we felt, as I had been one whole week studying night and day, I was getting sick of it: but thank goodness that part of it is over. He then inoculated us underneath the collar bone. Oh my! Wasn't it tender afterwards, I could hardly bear the weight of my clothes on it, it was just like a boil. To morrow night we have to go and get inoculated again. We have to have three inoculations.

We got our pass-ports the other day. I wish you could see the questions we have to fill in. I hate to begin at them. We have to state the colour of our hair and eyes. Our height, and weight. The shape of our nose and face and forehead and a dozen others. We have to have our pictures taken too, of course we only had two pictures, one to carry with us and one to stick on the passport which has to be sent on by mail. These passports cost $2.50 and our pictures $1.50 for two. There is an awful lot of red tape to go through before we can leave. It seems they are more than particular. We are going down to Mrs. Browning's this afternoon to fill in our passports, I expect we shall have 5 o'clock tea again. When we are ready to leave I shall wire you so don't get uneasy if you see Dolph[2] coming.

Vince and I were down to Julie Pines' night before last,

2. Perhaps the local mailman.

had cabbage and potatoes. Reta and Miss Baldwin came there too and Mrs. Jessie Pike and Llew Pike. We spent a pleasant afternoon. We went right up to the Hospital with Ret. I got home just eleven o'clock on the dot. Our lights are to be out at eleven: but we sometimes go over that.

—

Oct. 31[st.] Tuesday night.

Yesterday I was up to Mr. Brinton's to one o'clock dinner. Immediately after dinner I had to go to Holloway's studio[3] and get my two pictures and take them with my passport back again to Mr. Brinton's to get signed. After that I had to go to the Colonial Secretary's[4] office and hand it over to him. I then had to step into a store and get weighed and then go, oh! so far down to Mrs. Browning's to put down my weight. She wasn't at home, was out to the Consumptive Camp — Jensen's Camp.[5] So I wrote a letter and left it on the reception table for her.

All the money Phil Jensen has been collecting, he

3. A St. John's photographic studio operated by Robert Holloway and his sister Elsie. A member of the Newfoundland Regiment, he was killed April 14, 1917.
4. Sir John Robert Bennett. Before he entered politics was President and Managing Director of E.W.Bennett and Company.
5. Phil Jensen of Harbour Breton (about three hours from Belleoram by sea in those days) went overseas with 13th Battalion Royal Highlanders of Canada. He was gassed and severely wounded by shrapnel and spent three months in hospital. On his return to Newfoundland, he travelled around the island recruiting and raising money for the Red Cross. The camp for returned soldiers was named Jensen Camp. He later entered the ministry and was Rector of a parish in Baltimore, Maryland. His brother, Arthur, joined the Bank of Montreal and later became its president.

hands it over to Mrs. Browning. They have built a camp for those who are in the first stages of consumption. It is a flat roofed building. On the front is a Sunshine Room. This room is painted pale green or pea green with white windows. There is also a small dressing room, and a Nurse's home a few yards away. Mrs. Browning took Miss Janes and me there in her auto. We went all through the camp and Nurse's Home. Jensen's Camp is going to be written in green on white for the outside.

I was inoculated again last night, and dear me, haven't I been feeling miserable today. I got up to dress; but had to lie back again and didn't get up until nearly twelve. The inoculation went all over my system. The vaccination and the first inoculation did not take: but this one did, and I am told the third one is still worse. He inoculated me in the same spot, and it wasn't got quite over the first time. I am glad it has taken though.

The Portia sails to-morrow. I asked Tryphie to call for some things I wanted to send home: but she did not come. I did so want to send Aunt Suse's boots. I have not put them on since. I shall send them by parcel post.

Vince just rung me up. I told him I wasn't well and was going to bed early. I shall see him some time to mor-row. How did Rhynie like her hat? Is Art and they[6] back from St Pierre yet?

I shall get inoculated again next Monday night. I just dread it. Anyhow that is the last time. I haven't heard from Miss Janes to day. I expect she is feeling the effects of it too, or else she would have been down. There is quite a bit of work to go through in this business.

---

6. Typical Belleoram expression meaning "Art and his buddies or his mates."

We can do our own washing and ironing. I have washed once, and never ironed that for ever so many days after.

We make our own beds. Our meals are breakfast 8 o'clock, dinner one, supper 6, except on Sundays then it is five. We have a cup of tea and some bread and butter before going to bed on Saturday and Sunday nights.

I am going out to see Virtue[7] as soon as I feel well enough.

Vince had an awful cold last night when he was down here.

I wish I could get a chance to send some of my stuff home.

I cannot write any more. Remember me to Bish. I was thinking perhaps she would write.

Good Bye Mother.
From your daughter Fanny.

—

Mrs. Matilda Cluett
Belleoram
Newfoundland[8]

pleasure to get home any more, there is nothing or very little I leave behind. Lil can have the organ and you are to

7. Taylor who married a Ryan from St. John's and lived there for a number of years.
8. Portion missing but clearly she is discussing the disposal of her personal effects in the event of her death. Envelope is addressed to her mother and postmarked November 4, 1916.

have the rest I own; you may give Bish some of the photos I have around: but I hope and trust, God willing, that I shall get back again. Oh Yes! I forgot, if I don't come back, give Win one of those little centre tables of mine in the parlour.

I don't think I shall write any more.

Don't write to me mother, as I don't know where to tell you to address my letters.

The stuff I leave to you mother, you can do just what you like with it. Give Aunt Suse something. To-morrow Miss Elliott and I are going to the Museum. I don't think I shall go down to Mrs. Browning's on Tuesday.

> Good Bye Mother,
> From Your daughter Fanny

—

Wed

Dear Mother.

My underclothing has to be plain with no embroideries at all on it: so I've got to rip off the embroidery on the one Lil gave me.

Do you think you could manage to send me a gray striped flannelette petticoat in place of that old short one I bought, or never mind, I'll see if I can get one in town: but don't suppose I can get one. Our night dresses have to be quite plain. I have enough petticoats.

I bought a new pair of boots, so do not wear Aunt Suse's at all. Will send them as soon as I possibly can by parcel post.

I was vaccinated the other night, Monday night. It has started to itch today. He gave me two very large scratches.

I've got to get a thick bath robe.

Good Bye Mother.

Don't forget about the petticoat. Our underclothing has to be warm and plain.

It is raining cats and dogs. We had thunder and lightning last night. One of the girls got afraid and asked to sleep with me. I had the nightmare something dreadful.

I bought a pair of new overshoes and boots.

From your daughter Fanny.

—

I had to stop. Miss Janes came in discussing nursing.

Good Bye Mother.

Hotel Martha Washington
29 East 29th Street
New York

Wednesday night, Nov.15/16

Dear Mother,

Well! here I am in New York. We left North Sydney about 9:30 p.m Sunday night. Ida[1] and Phoebe came to the station with me. I thought to see Aunt Suse's Johnnie while in Sydney: but couldn't.

We arrived at Truro next morning: but hadn't delayed long enough to write home. We just had breakfast and started off again. The train got in St John[2] about 5 o'clock that evening. A gentleman whom we met on the train gave us a dinner at the restaurant on the station. He was very kind indeed. He said he would call us up at Martha Washington Hotel when he got in New York; but we haven't heard a word from him since. I guess he was glad to get rid of such a crowd. He was born in England, but has lived for a long time in New York. I think he travels a great deal. When in New York he stays at Sir John Howley's. We had to take a car from the North Station to the South Station in time for the mornings train to New York. At the South Station the porter told us the train was

---

1. Ida Cluett.
2. Meaning Saint John, New Brunswick.

33

going to leave at five minutes past ten and it was then twenty minutes to ten. We got a lunch and eat it just as fast as ever we possibly could. We were hurrying so much that when we got on the car we forgot to pay as we went in and had to bundle out on the porch again. When we got out there we had no American money and they would not take Canadian. However between us we got through.

Just as Miss Gallishaw[2] was stepping in the car, it started to go with a jerk. Well! my goodness sake, down she goes plump in the car. Her suitcase went one way, her interesting book that she had been lugging about with her everywhere went another way. I shall never forget it as long as I live.

We arrived at Central Station, New York Tuesday night at five o'clock. We had to go to see about our trunks being taken down to the boat, and then we had to try to get to this hotel. While we were talking about our trunks to the ticket agent, he said there was a man from this hotel outside to take people who wish to room there. He went out and brought him in for us; but we wouldn't take him at first; but he showed us the sign he wears inside of his hat with the name of this hotel on it. However we followed him. Miss Hewett[3] said if we didn't soon get there

---

2. Henrietta Gallishaw, a VAD, the daughter of the St. John's Harbour Pilot and sister of John Gallishaw who wrote *Trenching in Gallipoli*, S.B.Gundy, 1916.

3. Alice Hewitt, from Portsmouth, England, a trained nurse and head nurse at the Asylum for the Insane, later the Waterford Hospital, was travelling back to England with them. In England she married Newfoundland doctor James Knight who was attached to the Regiment as a medical officer. Later the couple moved back to Newfoundland where they raised three children.

she was going to hire a taxi; but we did not have to wait long afterwards. I was so glad.

We are travelling in care of Miss Hewett, a nurse from the asylum. Her home is in Portsmouth, England. The Government got her out here to work in Newfoundland. She was there nearly four years, and is now returning home; the government is paying her through. She intended to travel by way of Quebec; but Mrs. Browning liked for us to come this way, and of course Miss Hewett altered her plans, which was good of her.

Boston is nothing to New York. We have certainly travelled up and down Fifth Avenue.

I was in one store to day. Really I thought to myself that the floor we were on was nearly as large as half of Belleoram. I never would in all my life imagine anything like it. We went to the Hippodrome last night. I cannot begin to tell the most wonderful things we saw there.

I wish I had got Gab Cluett's address before I left home.

We have seen some of the skyscrapers. Boston seems like nothing now.

This morning we had to go down to the British Consul's office and show our passports and fill out an application. The other evening we went to the American Line office to get our tickets on the steamer St. Paul. The agent told us he would send them up that night. Well, we have waited for them all day to day, and they haven't come yet. It isn't all play for those who intend to take up this work.

Last night Molly Shea came on from St. John's, going

to England to be bridesmaid for her friend. Just think, anybody can afford to go to England just to be a bridesmaid. She was educated over there. Yesterday we met Miss Fitzgerald who has been to Bordeaux, war nursing. We shall be leaving New York on Saturday the 18th on the S.S. St. Paul, an American boat.

Before we left St. Johns', we were taken up to the Government House to meet Lady Davidson. She was very, very nice.

I shall never go across country again. I can't forget that awful ride.

We certainly have been doing some walking and riding since Thursday a week ago to-day. Miss Gallishaw's back is beginning to get a bit tired. Three of us woke up the other morning with great dark circles under our eyes. I guess we were beginning to get a bit jaded. We had so many things with us, that if we lost them it would be a terrible thing. There was our passports, our sleeping tickets, our travelling tickets, our money, our trunk checks. We shall have a rest when we get on the boat. I shall wire you when I arrive in London.

How did Lil like her coat? Did the switch[4] match her hair.

I wish you could see the inside of this hotel. There are two writing tables in this room. All the girls are gone to the theatre except me. Miss Janes is staying with her friends in Brooklyn. Our room is on the twelfth floor. Miss Gallishaw and Miss Hewett and I occupy one room. Miss Bartlett and Miss Shea another room.

---

4. A hairpiece to elongate hair or to make a bun.

When we go out, we keep tabs on each other. We never lose sight of each for a minute. You cannot imagine what New York is like.

I cannot write any more. I wrote a letter to Aunt Sarah Rose.

Good Bye Mother,

From Your daughter Fannie.

U.S.M.S. "St. Paul".

Friday morning
Nov.24/16

Dear Mother,

We are nearing our journey's end, or I suppose we are. Sunday morning we shall be in Liverpool. I think we are going to stay there until Monday morning. I know we shall be a long time getting through with our luggage and our passports at Liverpool, as they are very particular. We are not allowed to post our letters ashore that we write on this boat, we must mail them on the boat.

This is a beautiful day. Yesterday it was raining nearly all day. We haven't seen any land since Saturday, only the sky and water for miles on either side. The ship is rolling so much to day. I can hardly keep upright. This is the worst day we have had yet, as regards lop. I tell you she is certainly doing some rolling now. We have had splendid weather so far. I have not been a bit seasick, no more than if I was on the land. The bugle has just called all passengers to eleven o'clock chicken broth on the deck. I am not going out to get any to day, as I want to finish this letter.

Breakfast is served in the dining room from 8 a.m. until 10 a.m. Chicken broth is served at 11 a.m. on the deck. Luncheon at 1 o'clock. Tea and cakes and biscuits at 4 o'clock. Dinner at 7 o'clock. In fact breakfast and luncheon are dinners too, as there are so many, many courses. I cannot begin to tell you the kind of meals are served on this boat. First of all you can have whatever kind of fruit you want, then whatever kind of porridge you want, then eggs made up into different ways. Fish of different kinds. All kinds of meat that can be mentioned nearly. Different kinds of salads and puddings and French pastry. Ice cream served in the most beautiful ways I ever saw. Sometimes it is brought in the shape of a cake, and a rose, and oh so many beautiful ways. I wonder whatever kind of a cook they have. We have four knives and three forks and three or four spoons every meal. It is wonderful. You could never believe there are so much food cooked at one meal. I wonder what they do with what is left over. One half of the world don't know how the other half lives. When we were down to St. Keels[1] this summer; if we had had only a little bit of this, how we would have enjoyed it. Now this morning I couldn't eat my mutton chop, nor American Dry Hash, nor Graham muffin. I didn't want any honey or marmalade nor Blackcurrant conserve and so many things more. I think Miss Janes would exchange it all for brews and fish.[2] One soon gets sick of so much. I have had chicken so many times, that I don't want that any more. When you look at the menu card you don't know where to look to first. The other night I had raw oysters served on their shells. First of all a soup plate was

---

1. A favourite fishing spot for trout and salmon between Belleoram and Pool's Cove.
2. Fish and brewis (hardtack or ship's biscuit soaked and then boiled) is the traditional Newfoundland dish born first of necessity and then custom and then delight.

covered with ice, then the shells laid on the ice, and right in the middle of the dish, there was a little glass of tomato dressing. The way the dishes are made up is wonderful.

I did go up on the deck and get some soup served in bouillon cups. Miss Hewett came down after me.

We have not made many acquaintances on the boat. I met Mr. Senior from London and a Mr. Fox from some part of England. We have great games of cards. We play whist an awful lot. The Captain is a jolly man. The Countess of Limerick is on board. She seems to keep in the back ground. She has a woman travelling with her. They both dress plainly. Her maid is better looking than herself. You would never know she was a Countess if you weren't told. There are quite a few swell people going across. I wish you could see this room I am writing in. The floor is covered with the loveliest red and yellow carpet. The ceiling is slate or buff colour. The walls are cream and ornamented beautifully. There are six writing desks. This paper is free. There is also a great glass case containing 1177 English books, and 217 French, and 50 from the London Times Works. There are special hours to get these books from the deck steward.

The seats here are padded so thickly that it is solid comfort. You nearly sink down into them.

The dining room contains nearly forty tables. You cannot imagine the size of it. Each table would seat, well I don't know how many. Six people can sit at the very smallest. Fifteen and so on sit at some of them. During luncheon and dinner the orchestra plays all the time. There is a piano in the dining room, one in the sitting room, and one in the hall.

We do not have coffee in the dining room at 7 o'clock; but wait until we go to the sitting room, then we begin to play whist and order coffee. I wish you could see some of the tables, the ladies drinking coffee, playing checkers, smoking cigarettes and talking, and dressed in silks and laces. At night the diamonds are worn. I looked at the Countess' rings last night. Dear me I never saw such a display of jewellery in all my life as I have seen this week. I never thought I would see life as it is. I only wish Bish and Lil could take a peep into the sitting room at night. There is a concert to night in the dining room. Miss Hewitt is going to recite "I miss you." I was asked to sing and refused.

Yesterday morning and night before last I was suffering with the same old thing. I couldn't get up for breakfast.

We were in New York from Tuesday night until Saturday noon. I suppose you wonder where I got the money to pay my way through. We were given $75 besides our travelling ticket as far as Liverpool.

Out of that $75.00 we paid our bill at Washington Hotel. That didn't come to very much as three of us took a room together. So our bed room only cost us $4.50 each. Well! We had to pay for our meals extra, and after every meal we tipped the waitress five or ten cents each. Our expenses to get to the S.S. Paul[3] were around 60 cents each. At the Consul's office we had to pay 50 cts each. Our sleepers on the train were expensive. We have to pay out of it our own way from Liverpool to London; but I think that is about seven dollars, so you see we have got to be spending all the time. We changed our American money

---

3. Meaning the SS *St. Paul*.

on this ship into English money. We have had as much changing of money, from Canadian into American and from American into British. I have now quite a few £s in gold and some British notes. Oh yes! we have to pay for our Uniforms after we get across.

I bought a cream flannel collar in New York. I don't care much about it now. Tell Lil I will send [it] to her when I get settled in London. I had a pair of white chamoisette gloves $1.00, and a black velvet sailor hat $1.00. I went to several shows in New York.

Miss Janes had no board to pay in New York as she stayed with friends.

We get the war news every day by wireless. Miss Janes bought her snap shot with her; but was told she cannot do any thing towards taking pictures. One has to be very careful. To night and to-morrow we are what they call in the war zone. People will have their life belts and money near them to night. In fact, I have known right where to lay my hand on my bath robe and life belt. I don't think I shall take any of my clothes off to night. The steamer went a great way off her course we are told to cheat the submarines. There is such a swell on now, I cannot see what one will do if we had to get out in the boats. We sleep on the third floor. I like to see you mother trying to find your way around. There are so many halls and pairs of stairs. I cannot write any more now. Good Bye. From Your daughter Fannie. I cannot tell you where to write in London as we may be shifted. Get George Dicks[4] address for me.

---

4. A Belleoram soldier with the Newfoundland Regiment.

Queen Mary's Hostel for Nurses
40, Bedford Place,
London. W. C.
Wednesday night.
Nov 29/16

Dear Mother,

Did you get the message I sent you from London the first night I arrived here. It was dated Nov. 27th I think, or 26th. I couldn't send many words as it cost me a shilling a word, even for your name and address and for my name and address, so you know I could not send many words. We were nine days coming from New York to Liverpool. We left New York Saturday at noon and arrived in Liverpool Sunday evening about 4 o'clock. We went to one boarding house and were told it was filled and were told to go just a little way down the street. We got there. It was called Barry Hotel and no doubt but what it was Barry Hotel. We had supper in a small room where there was a man smoking all the time in his shirt sleeves. We had bread and butter for tea. The bread was cut into little thin half slices and already buttered. We had a little bit of marmalade in our dish which was supposed to do for the jolly crowd of us. Of course you know there were five of us. Miss Henrietta Gallishaw, Miss Clare Janes, Miss Bertha Bartlett,[1] and Miss Alice Hewett

---

1. Sister of Captain Bob Bartlett and Lieutenant Rupert Bartlett, Newfoundland Regiment, a VAD from Brigus.

with whom we were travelling. When we finished supper we started off for St Paul's Cathedral: but am sorry to say that the services were over, being at 3 p.m. instead of 6 p.m. as we thought. However, we went into another church, the oldest church of all. There were very few people there. Only males in the choir, no girls at all. A real low church. The hymns are exactly like ours, numbers and everything. The church is very grand inside. The work of it is so beautiful. We sang "God save the King" the very first thing of all. One of the hymns was "Holy Father in thy mercy", and another "Thou art coming oh my Saviour." Of course they sing the psalms and every thing. I cannot stand to hear the psalms sung; that is why I did not care to go to the Cathedral in St John's. I preferred St Thomas' Church.[2]

We have had business to go to Devonshire House[3] three times since we came to London. It was the Duke of Devonshire's House, and he gave it over for this work. I just wish you could get a peep there. I have only been in the Reception Room: but Miss Gallishaw who had our papers, had to go into another. There are two great big fire places in the Reception Hall, and sixteen great pillars, eight on either side, running the length of the room, and a famous oil painting over one mantel piece. The tables have wonderful legs, all heavy brass and carved out to beat the

2. The old Garrison church in the east end of St. John's, generally known as displaying less ornate furnishings and symbolism as compared to, for example, the Cathedral which was generally considered "higher" church, although these comparisons are less obvious now. However, they must have been in Fanny's day; or at least they were to her.
3. Built in the Palladian style, it was located on Piccadilly Ave. in the heart of London, between the corners of Berkeley Street and Stratton Street It was the London residence of the Dukes of Devonshire whose family name was Cavendish.

band, and marble topped. These are three great big enormous glass doors opening out of the Reception Room into the front of the Mansion. Inside, there are three large openings showing the magnificent winding stairway. I never thought I would ever see the like.

The first time we went there, we went in a taxi, from the Pay and Record Office. Capt. Timewell[4] sent Stan Harvey (Dr Harvey's[5] son in St Johns') with us. He then went to Euston Station and got all our luggage and had it brought to this place. We have had many a ride in a taxi.

When Capt. Timewell was at the Pay and Record Office, I enquired about George Dicks. Of course I had a look at the book, and saw his mother was Martha Dicks, so I knew that was the George Dicks I was looking for. I was sorry to find he had left London shortly before we got here and is now at Ayr.[6] Had he still been at the Hospital I was going to see him. We are getting passes to night to go to Wandsworth Hospital to morrow. I had a letter to take to Neal Pike;[7] but I found also that he is gone to Ayr.

This is a swell place we are now staying. Of course we haven't anything to pay here, it is especially for Colonial Nurses. No one from England I hear is supposed to stay.

---

4. Henry Arthur Timewell, a chartered accountant, was Regimental paymaster in Great Britain for the Newfoundland Regiment.

5. Dr. Alfred Harvey was a "particularly brilliant" physician, accoucheur and diagnostician in St. John's attached to the Forest Road Hospital, later the General Hospital.

6. Ayr, Scotland, where the Newfoundland Regiment was training.

7. Frederick Neil Pike of St. John's, the brother of Emily Pike who boarded the *Portia* with Fanny at St. Lawrence; Fanny and her family also knew Jessie and Llew Pike of St. John's. R.G. Pike was the Belleoram manager for Harvey's who lived in St. John's but visited Belleoram frequently in the course of his duties.

The first we arrived, the porter rushes out to the taxi saying, "Are you from South Africa?" It would make a cat laugh. They had been expecting twenty seven nurses from South Africa just at the time we arrived; they came later. Just as we were coming down stairs, they were all flocking in, in two's and three's, wearing dark blue uniforms and white panama hats. You can imagine what they looked like, so many of them and dressed alike. They seem to be well educated, and speak so nicely. Their indoor uniform is cream linen, some wear the shoulder cape.

Mrs. Kerr Lawson is mistress of this place. I don't know if she was a titled lady before she undertook this work or not. I imagine she was. In the evening she wears a black satin dress with a train, low neck with queer shaped beads, and a beautiful long cape. Oh so stately; but so kind to everyone. We go to her when we want to know any thing. There is another girl, who stays with Mrs. Kerr Lawson. At dinner time she wears a blue velvet dress trimmed with brown fur.

This house is an enormous size. There are numerous rooms in it. This writing room is down the basement, and opening out of this room is a billiard room with six great electric lights over the table. I think of Bish's light down the shop over the table. Of course this billiard table is not used, but always covered over. It seems as though this house must have been handed over for this work since the war. Perhaps Mrs. Kerr Lawson owns it herself. In this writing room, there are four of the loveliest little round tables, with carved mahogany legs and green baize tops you ever saw. I expect they cost a dollar each. In the centre is a long writing table with the most beautiful inkstand I ever saw. It holds two inkstands, but is so heavy, that I could hardly lift it off the table with two hands. There are three lovely morocco arm chairs and oh dear! every kind of a chair to make one comfortable. Yesterday we were taken around "St John's Gate". It is very very old. To go through it makes you feel as if you were in Jerusalem somewhere. In one room there is [a] great oil painting of Queen Victoria and King Edward, full length. I cannot tell you what is there, only I know everything connected with olden times. The stairway is solid oak, but so old. We are asked to go there to morrow to see Lady Perrot. I do not want to go; but I suppose we shall have to. That building is used for Red Cross Work. In the store room, there are thousands of parcels to be sent to different parts. In the Library there are hundreds of "First Aid Books" like mine in all languages.

On Dec. 6th we are to go to Lincoln Hospital, 4th Northern General Hospital. Miss Janes cannot go until 20th of Dec. We have our out door great coat uniform, of dark grey material. I had to get mine shortened, as they have to be 6 inches from the ground. It cost me just £5 exactly. I had a dozen aprons, ½ doz prs of cuffs, 1/4 doz collars, studs, handkerchiefs for caps, three dresses. I had one dress ready made, and had to get two made, as the sleeves were a bit short.

I had to leave off and go upstairs to the dining room to get the regular 8:30 cup of tea, and I did certainly enjoy it; we don't get much tea.

—

Thursday night.

This morning we visited Wandsworth Hospital. Miss Gallishaw wanted to see a young man in Ward B. We got out passports from Pay and Record Office before starting. Wandsworth Hospital has a numerous lot of wards. We had quite a bit of walking to do before we got to Ward B. Miss Gallishaw had no trouble then to find him. He had had a gun shot wound in [the] thigh, but is doing splendidly. In the hall we met a fellow from Bonne Bay. We know who are N.F.L.Drs by the Caribou emblem. We have to get ours from N.F.L.D. Mr. Morgan is sending there for them for us. We have bought our Ward shoes which cost 9s [shillings] per pair. We have our shoulder bandages and hat bandages and arm bandages. Everything seems to be very expensive in London. Miss Gallishaw had to pay 9d [pence] 3/4 for a small package of bone hair pins.

I tell you it sometimes is a bother figuring up the £ and farthings. When we ride on the bus it is sometimes a penny and sometimes 3d and sometimes 2d. It is great sport. One of the four of us will pay for us all, then when we get home we have to settle up what we owe each other. You can imagine the sport we have. Sometimes when we come from shopping we have to get pencil and paper and reckon our poor brains especially when our goods are put on one bill.

Did I tell you we are going to Lincoln Hospital on Wednesday next to the North. This evening we went to Westminster Abbey. It was so impressive.

Queen Mary's Hostel for Nurses
40, Bedford Place,
London. W. C.
Dec. 5/16
Tuesday morning

Dear Lil,

I just this minute finished writing Bish, and while waiting for Luncheon bell, I thought I'd start a letter to you: but
I cannot say what time it will be finished; as this afternoon
Miss Gallishaw and I are going out to the zoo, and then to
"Pay and Record Office", and Miss Gallishaw wants to go
to a Jewellry [sic] Store to get the chain on her glasses mended. She has given me a leather wristlet and I think I'll get the
face taken off my watch now as long as she was so kind as
to give me the wristlet. Miss Janes went away yesterday
evening with some South African "Sisters". They have gone
to some swell house. I know they will have a rich time. They
are gone to Tablo, to Lord Beresford's house I think.[1] We
were going to the country a few days ago; but Mrs. Kerr
Lawson thought afterwards it wasn't worth while to send
us, as we had to go to our Hospital Dec. 6th, and it would
mean so much humbugging with our luggage.

---

1. Lord Charles William de la Poer Beresford was a colourful Conservative
MP for Portsmouth known for pushing the interests of the British Navy, in
which he had served with distinction. The Beresford family seat was on
the River Dove, a mile outside of the Derbyshire town, Hartington.

There is so much to tell, I scarcely know when and where to begin. Of course I cannot go into details about it; for it would take too much time and paper.

We had such a grand time from New York to Liverpool. We left as you know New York on Saturday at noon and arrived in Liverpool the next Sunday week about 11 a.m. I wasn't the least bit sea sick, no more than if I had been on the land. The last couple of days we were out it was a bit rough. There were some very high seas, or at least I thought they were enormous. When we were passed the danger line, then that night we were told of it. I did not know there was one spot more dangerous than another: but I find at 8 a.m. on Saturday morning I think it was that that was where the Lusitania[2] was torpedoed. We were also told that mines were undoubtedly driven in around the Irish Coast: oh my! we did not know what minute we were going to strike one; but we were told there was not much danger of being torpedoed as the sea was too rough for them; that you can imagine was good news. I knew just where to lay my hand on the life buoy. It was interesting to watch a steamer away in the distance signaling the St. Paul.

One of the "South African Sisters" was telling us the other night of her trip from France to London. She came across on a troop ship, and there were heaps of gold too. Of course the Germans knew of that ship; and she said

---

2. A Cunard ocean liner from Britain sunk by a German submarine in May 1915. All 1,201 passengers aboard, including 128 Americans, were lost in a strike that violated the traditional rules of submarine warfare. This caused a diplomatic disaster for German relations in the United States. The destruction of American shipping led to the United States declaration of war on Germany in April 1917.

the captain told them when they were safe that there had been a submarine before them all the time; but they had so many boats guarding them, that that saved them from being torpedoed. That would certainly have been a treat to have got hold of that transport ship.

One nurse here last night was telling us of her experience in Russia. It is only now that we know anything of Russia, France, South Africa etc. The South African Sisters were at first going to Salonica; but now they are going to France. It is frightfully cold there. They have their kit bags: they use them for beds, and then there are parts that serve for baths etc. They are very convenient.

I do hope they won't send us to France the winter. I know from what the others say I would certainly freeze to death.

It cost us 16/3 coming from Liverpool to London and that was travelling 3rd class. The trains are divided into little narrow rooms with a seat on either side, each seat to hold about four. It is quite comfortable. Third class is good enough for anybody.

We shall be starting off to-morrow for our Hospital at Lincoln, so I have to do more packing again tonight. We shall leave London on the 11:45 a.m. train and arrive there around 4. p.m.

We have been given tickets for theatres quite often. The first night we arrived here His Majesty sent tickets for us to go to Queen's Hall[3] to hear famous music and

---

3. Completed in 1893, Queen's Hall was a classical music concert auditorium located three blocks north of Oxford Circus in Langham Place. The building was known for its excellent acoustics. The St. George's Hotel is now located on the old Queen's Hall site.

singing. I was telling Bish about it on her letter. We have also gone to see "Peg O' my Heart", and "The Widows Might" and "Romance".

To night at dinner time we were wondering if we were going to be given any more tickets. By and by in comes Miss Walmesley with some paper and a pencil; that of course was a good sign; but Great Scott, she walked past our table and went up to the African Sisters and got their names for the theatre; but thank goodness she stopped at our table on her way down and asked who would like to go to the theatre; but she said there were only two tickets left; so what were we going to do. Miss Gallishaw said for me to go; but afterwards I told her to go; so of course she is going. I would like to have gone but then someone had to stay back. For once I saw Miss Janes had gone and Miss Bartlett had made a date for this evening with Mr. Janes: but Miss LeMessiurer, a friend of Miss Gallishaws who came to day, took the second ticket. I wish she had not come, for then Miss Gallishaw and I would have gone. Miss LeMessiurer[4] from St Johns has been over here nursing for quite a while. She had two weeks leave off, so spent one week down at some wealthy family's. There are only just a few of them in [the] family; but they keep eleven girls; so you can imagine what kind of a house it was.

I am sending some postal cards of the Tower of London, where we went last Saturday. That is the place to see. We were shown in the room where the two young princes were murdered. It is a little small room. We

4. Likely Isabel LeMessurier.

peeped in the cell where Sir Walter Raleigh was confined. We stood on the spot where so many have been executed. We saw the block and axe. We went in the room where those four bishops were imprisoned. We then went in where all the armour of Henry VII and VIII are kept. Great Scott, I never saw the like of it. Such a lot of swords, and pistols, and guns, and revolvers: the Roman shields, armour of every description.

We went into the House of Parliament around ten o'clock in the morning. We are admitted on Saturday mornings only. The suffragettes[5] made it hard for the women to go through. I only wish you could go through Westminster Abbey. There are statues of every King and Queen and famous man that ever lived. We visited the tombs of the old Kings and Queens. We were shown Edward I tomb; it was the longest there. You know he was called Longshanks.

I went to St Paul's Cathedral on Sunday morning to 10:30 prayers and received Holy Communion. There were seven ministers there. Four administered the Sacrament. I won't begin to tell what that building was like. We sat the eighth seat down from the chancel; and you could not tell whether the ministers were facing you or back on. The chancel is like a small church.

It is such a long time since I have heard any news from home. My address will be 4th Northern General

---

5. Female political protesters in the early twentieth century who aggressively lobbied governments to give women the right to vote. In Newfoundland, Armine Gosling founded the Women's Franchise League in 1920. In 1925 the Newfoundland Legislature passed a bill allowing women over twenty-five years of age the right to vote.

Hospital. Lincoln. England. Tell mother I am quite well. Had to get a hot water bottle.

Very cold.

Fan.

England
Lincoln,
Bishops Hostel,
Dec. 31st, 1916.

Sunday morning

Dear Mother,

As I had a couple of hours leisure this morning, I thought I would drop you a few lines. I haven't heard a word from home since the week before I left St. John's, N.F.L.D.

I am going to tell you a little about our work. We are called at half past five in the morning; but I always wait until six or five minutes past; then of course we have to rush as we must be in our wards at seven o'clock. It is cold in the mornings dressings [*sic*]. I wish you could see me hurrying. We have half an hour to breakfast. Sometimes we get in a quarter to seven, that leaves us fifteen minutes for breakfast. On Xmas morning we didn't have to go to breakfast until seven o'clock instead of half past six, which meant we could stay a little longer in bed. I just got in the dining room in time to drink a little tea and get a bit of bread and butter; so you can see the longer time they have given us the worse we are.

Miss Gallishaw rooms with me, she got up to go to 7 o'clock Mass. We were supposed to go to 6 o'clock Holy Communion in the little Church by the Hospital, but I didn't go. I was sorry afterwards that I didn't go. Miss Gallishaw said she will never forget Xmas morning. The patients crippled out to go to Mass. Poor things, some of them just can manage to get around on their crutches, and yet they managed to get out to Mass at 7 o'clock. When it is seven o'clock here it is just four in N.F.L.D. When we go to our hospital in the mornings at 6 o'clock, you people are sleeping away quite comfortable. Some mornings it is raining pell mell and dark as pitch nearly: other mornings when it isn't foggy the moon and stars are so bright. The other morning when I went into our ward I said "Good Night" to them instead of Good Morning. It was just the same as starting work after supper. The patients laughed. They knew there was not much morning about it.

At 7 o'clock exactly, a "Sister in Charge" knocks on one of the tables as a signal for everybody to stand for prayers. We say the Lords Prayer altogether, and she says a blessing, and that is all there is to it. I sit down again after prayers to finish my piece of bread or my tea, but we are not supposed to do it. You see we should get to the dining room by half past six, and that would give us half an hour for breakfast; but we don't do it. I don't like the idea of getting up so early. You know we have a mile to walk for our breakfast from the Hostel to the Hospital. Miss Gallishaw and I take turns in getting up to light the gas in the mornings. We have many a laugh over it.

When we arrive at our huts, which would be about five minutes past seven, we put on our caps and aprons and belts, turn up our sleeves. I have the centre of the ward, the other two nurses have the sides. I first of all scrub "Sisters" tables, then I go to the patients' dining table and scrub that, and then four long benches, then I come to the other end of the ward and scrub another long white table and four benches. Then if it is my week to do the laundry I begin sorting that, so as to have it ready for the orderly to take to the laundry.

Then the patients who are feeling extra well begin to sweep, one each side of the ward. After they have I dust all the middle. Then when that is finished I take two clean towels down to the pantry, and bring up two others, then I wash the two dirty ones and put them on a clothes horse by one of the stoves to dry: then it is time to fill the jugs full of hot water, and have soap and towel ready. When this is done it is nine o'clock, our lunch hour. I have that same thing to do every morning Sundays and all. I never know it is Sunday, except when somebody mentions it. These things have to be done. The wards must be spotlessly clean, owing to so many bad wounds. We have half an hour to lunch. Our huts are not joined on to the Hospital. After lunch we start getting ready for dressings. No more scrubbing until next morning except the pantry and bathrooms to be kept clean. For the dressings we screen the patients, get fomentations ready, sterilize all instruments. At half past ten get lunches ready for patients. They have a mug of hot milk for lunch.

About half past twelve dinner is brought to the hut from the cook house for the patients. Patients who are unable to cut their dinner, we cut it up for them, some have meat and some fish. I usually go to the dining room for o'clock dinner which is another half hour. In the afternoons there are washings of face and hands and backs and bed making. At four lunch again for patients, which means special tea for bed patients and tea from cook house for the smart ones. By special tea I mean, I make it if I am on duty in a tea pot, good and strong. I don't suppose it can be very good which comes from the cook house in a great big tin coffee can.

Five o'clock is our lunch half hour. From that time on until eight dressings again and a general clean up of the ward before leaving for the night. We have three hours off duty every day, and sometimes we have extra time off duty. Yesterday morning I came off at nine o'clock and didn't go on again until three in the afternoon, but you see we have to walk back and forth from the Hostel to the Hospital for our meals. We have half a day off every week, and one whole day a month. Next Thursday I shall have been here a month, then we are asked to sign on again, for however long we wanted to.

The fifth day when I was helping "Sister" with the dressings, I fainted away. When I came to myself I was stretched out on the floor. I tell you I have seen some horrible wounds. I often have to turn my head and look out through the window.

While we are on duty, and especially in the afternoon, we are certainly rushed. For five or six hours we don't stop hardly to draw breath. I am on duty this afternoon and evening; but Nurse Fletcher is on too, so that will be a great help. Many a time I have been on alone, so you can imagine what a busy time I had, when there is sufficient work for two.

It is now twenty five minutes to twelve. I must close

and tidy myself a bit, as I have to go to the dining room for first dinner, and be on duty again by one o'clock. I have twenty minutes walk before me.

I had to buy two pair of wool bloomers. I am knitting myself a pair of black stockings. Good Bye Mother.

From Fanny.

Lincoln,
England
4th Northern Gen. Hospital
Jan.20/17

Dear Mother,

I received your letter & the Xmas cards a few days ago; you did not say if you had received any letters from Lincoln yet. I imagine the two you got were from London.

You spoke about how terrible it must be to see and hear bombs. I must tell you I have not yet witnessed one. We have not yet thank goodness been troubled with them since our arrival; but they have been expected. Of course people here are just ready for them; they have only just got to show themselves; and I verily believe they will soon be brought down. The sky is searched nearly every night. It looks very interesting to see the three searchlights examining the sky and recrossing each other. I just love to look at them.

I shall tell you a little of how our patients are getting on. Quite a few of them have gone convalescent since I came. One of them has been a soldier ever since he was able to become one. His father was also a soldier. He told me three of his brothers were killed in this war.

I never saw a man as he was for washing himself. I think he used to live in the bathroom shaving himself. After he had dressed in his uniform ready to go convalescent he did indeed look every inch a soldier. He was very tall, and of course looked very clean, the result of so much washing. How in the world he could be bothered with trying to keep himself spotless all the time I don't know. Whenever they leave the ward to go to a convalescent home, they always go around the ward to say good bye to the patients and nurses. Sniper Rosee is gradually getting better. He can't be any more than eighteen. I must ask him when I go on duty this afternoon. You see he was wounded in the spine and of course that meant paralysis. Just think of him lying in that bed for fifteen months, not able to walk a step; but I really believe he will in time to come. He goes through a process of electrical massage quite often, and of course that works the muscles and bones, and circulates the blood. The lady who treats him is really an expert; so I think he will pull through. He tried one day just to see if he could stand; but unfortunately he had no strength in his leg, and poor thing was compelled to sit down again. He is so patient lying there all day long. Some days we get him out in the big chair, and pull him to the stove. I ask him at times if he would like to sit up for a little while. He says "Nurse, I will be by and bye"; so you can see he does not feel much like sitting up.

The orderly sometimes takes him to another ward to an entertainment. There have been concerts in the Recreation Room; well! Rosee is put in the wheel chair, and taken across; he is then lifted on the couch to amuse himself as well as he can. Every morning he is given the instruments, such as forceps, probes, scissors, etc to clean, and he does them well too. I wish you could see him half reclining in the bed polishing away at them. He is quite well from the lower part of his spine up, just as well as ever he was; but you know he looks very pale. He spends a great deal of his time sketching. I do wish you could see some of his drawings. He just loves to draw the nurses and soldiers. His sketches are indeed very interesting. He tells me he cannot do the faces good; but apart from that they are all right; and of course beneath each sketch there is a saying. It is amusing.

When I was giving him a blanket bath the other day, I touched his right foot; but he had no feeling there. I gradually went up his foot until I passed the ankle, there life started. Isn't it funny to think from the ankle down there is no life; that of course is the reason why he has to be massaged.

Lying next to him is a man named Inges. His arm was amputated this week to the elbow. He has had that arm bad for thirteen months, and after all the suffering he has gone through, it finally had to be amputated. I thought his arm was getting better; it surprised me very much when I heard Inges was preparing for operation. "Sister" told me yesterday to come with her while she was dressing it. I was doubtful at first whether I should bear the sight: but I nerved myself and bore the ordeal all right. Of course I could see nothing of the inside of the arm; but just where the flesh was pulled smoothly over the place it was cut and sewn together. It didn't look so frightfully bad at all. It bleeds quite a bit. Inges is a very nice man. I judge he is in his forties. We miss him so much around the stove; he always looked out to the kettles on the stove, and saw there was water in the sterilizer; and always helped to take the meals around to the other bed patients. He was a great help. I trust he will soon be able to get up again. After his operation, there was little difficulty in keeping him lying down. Sister told me to have an eye on him; I tell you he was strong to be forced back on his pillow. Of course he didn't know what he was doing; but that is all over now, and he can enjoy a laugh. The other boys call him "Dad" all the time. Every once in a while you will hear them say "Dad", what is this, and "Dad" what is that? One woman visitor kissed him I think she was his wife. I cannot write any more this morning. I must see about getting some dinner. Miss Gallishaw and I are off duty, and we do not intend to go back to the Hospital to dinner; but I hope the Matron will not find it out. We are going to boil some eggs, and make some toast and tea, and we have a jar of strawberry jam. Good Bye Mother.

From Your daughter Fanny.

Lincoln,
Feb. 25th/17

Sunday night

Dear Mother,

I received your two letters last week on same day: one was dated Jan. The other Feb.

Is it possible Rhynie is married, or have I mistaken the name. I shan't believe it until I get another letter. Tell Bish her letter was very interesting, and to try and write me again. You cannot realize mother how very welcome home letters are to us, who see no one but Canadians, Australians, Scotchman, Englishmen all day long.

You said something about sending me a cake. I should dearly love to have it: but I assure you mother the postage is not very small. Janes, Gallishaw and Bartlett have had eatables sent them from N.F.L.D, and the postage seemed almost too much, especially in war times. All we hear these days is "Economy in war times".

Oh Mother! We are put on rations. A 2 lb. loaf of bread must last us two days: and we are also given 3/4 lb. sugar to do us for a week. Each nurse was presented with a small bag to hold her loaf of bread and tin of sugar.

I did laugh the first morning these bags were given out. We all went up to one of the nurses in single file to get them. The bag that was given me was a funny coloured one, just an ordinary striped one. I didn't like it; so I managed to slip it on the table again behind some-body's back, and got in the row with the others again, and was lucky enough to get a rosy coloured one next time. Nobody saw me put away the other one. How we did laugh when I told Nurse Gallishaw of what I did.

—

Sunday. March 4th

I must tell you a little more about our rations. Sometimes my 2 lb loaf of bread lasts me for two days: but when we have an afternoon and evening off, I cannot make it do me; for then we make toast and of course we eat more.

It is laughable many a time since we have been rationed out. The other evening I went down to the dining room for my tea at 5 p.m., and all the bread I had was just a little bit of crust: so I put that in the corner of my coat pocket. We are so hungry sometimes, and yet we have only to allowance ourselves. It is like this, we cut off a small slice and look with downcast eyes to see how much there is left. You can imagine how much bread we can afford to eat at one meal out of a 2 lb loaf. We must eat off it for breakfast, lunch, dinner, tea and supper for two days. Fortunately I don't want any bread at dinner time.

As regards the sugar, I never have a bit left by the time Friday and Saturday get around.

Now this morning I had my porridge & tea without

sugar. Yesterday I had no sugar, and dear me, the puddings taste so raw without it.

We have to sweeten everything with that 3/4 lb. There is no sweetness put in anything, and I do like my tea etc so sweet, and to think I have to go two or three days without any.

While I am writing this; we chanced to be discussing the sugar problem. One of the nurses said, we do not get 3/4 but only 1/2. I thought it could never be 3/4.

I wish you could see us going to the hospital in the mornings. In one hand we have a case containing cuffs, collars, aprons, scissors, caps etc.

In the other hand we carry our ration bag, containing our 2 lb loaf, and our tin of sugar.

I was wondering where on earth I was going to get a tin to put my sugar into: when as luck would . . .[1]

—

Sunday March 11

. . . for then I am absolutely certain I may borrow from them. One or the other of us is constantly borrowing.

Our tea at 4:30 p.m. consists of bread and margarine. I don't think I should ever know the taste of good butter again. We never have anything but margarine. Last Sunday morning we had an egg for breakfast and again to day we had one.

One of the girls at my side of the table left, and the

---

1. Two pages are missing from original letters.

housekeeper put an egg for her last Sunday: but I tell you I got that egg with my own. You see she used to sit by me, and of course that place is now spread for her: I expect when Mrs. Blow finds out there is one short, she will want to know what became of that egg.

To day for dinner we had such a small helping of meat, and beans. Those who came in late got no beans, so they had potatoes instead. I could nearly have put my meat in my mouth at once.

I haven't tasted a bit of cabbage since I left N.F.L.D, neither pork. Sometimes I feel I could eat a boiler full.

Our pudding to day was made of sago and barley combined.

Yesterday for dinner I had no sugar, so Bartlett had some candy with her; and gave me one to stir in my pudding: the worst of all is when we have apple pie: dear me! I can tell you it's not just nice. I know I should not use so much the first part of the week; but there what can one do with only 3/4 of a lb, and to use it in everything.

One day in the week is a meat less day for us, or I should [say] two days: for on Tuesdays we have soup and potatoes, and on Friday we have fish and potatoes.

The other night one of the patients gave me a couple of scones for my tea; they tell us to have some of their bread; for they are allowed 2 lbs per day: it isn't any use to go to the stores to buy bread: they will not sell it to you; but they will sell sweet cakes.

It must cost an awful lot to run a hospital; for sometimes I take stock of the things, by looking round and taking in the items: There are nearly two hundred nurses in this hospital, and every two days, each one is supplied with a loaf of bread, and then take into consideration the number of potatoes they cook, and the amount of meat they cook, and the quantity of milk and margarine then is used everyday; but I would give it all for a square meal of pork and cabbage or beef and potatoes, or meat soup; and oh! I would so like to have potato cakes; however! I cannot get them, so must not complain.

I never felt better in health in my life except a cough I had when I left N.F.L.D. I still have it; but it does not hurt me. I never know what it is to feel a pain; of course we are tired at times; for we have a tremendous lot of walking to do. The wards are nearly twice the length of the Orange Hall, and one goes the whole of it about one hundred times per day.

The men's bathroom is down one end opposite the pantry, whereas all the medicines, towels, sheets, handkerchiefs, soap, bandages, are kept the other end; so you can imagine the walking there is to be done.

Sometimes when we are making special tea for the ward we have forgotten a spoon, down we trot to the pantry again; probably when we get up again, one of the patients wants a hot water bottle, down we go again, for they are kept in the pantry.

We had another convoy about a week ago. Two hundred came to this hospital: but we got only two. One of them is a T.B. patient (Tuberculosis). He was wounded in the thigh; quite a young boy; he is so pale looking. A few evenings ago I took his temperature which was over 100, and pulse 102: The next evening when I took it , it was a bit better, and yesterday evening it had gone down quite a bit.

The other evening a visitor came to see him; he handed me his pass: I saw he was a Jew; I thought the boy looked Jewish; you know no visitors are allowed into a hut without just showing their pass.

Groves has had to undergo another operation. I hear there are talks of sending him to his home in Canada. This morning sister was syringing his leg; then she put plugging into it. Plugging is put on one side of the leg, and pulled through the other side. It is awful.

Poor Rodgers has had his hip cut open again, to take a piece of bone that was floating around in the wound out: that wound is awfully deep.

Goswell is able to hop around the ward; I expect he will soon be sent to his home in London. He went yesterday down town to Theatre Royal. It seems so nice to see those poor things able to get up again.

Four have died in Gallishaw's ward.

I expect when you hear from me again, I shall be on night duty, that is go on 8:30 p.m. and come off 8:30 a.m.

Good Bye Mother;

From your loving daughter Fannie.

4th Northern General Hospital,
Lincoln, March 29th 1917.

Dear Mother,

I wrote you just a short while ago: but I didn't know then that I should be called on to go to France or abroad some-where. One morning at dinner, names were called to go abroad. Amongst them was mine. I wasn't at dinner at the time they were called: but Sister told me when she came back that she had something to tell me.

You can imagine the surprise I got. At five o'clock of same day, we met in sitting room of Hospital and were there questioned by matron as regards inoculation and vaccination. I am not to be done either with, as I was inoculated three times in October, and it is only four years ago that I was vaccinated: so I was jolly lucky wasn't I?

Janes and Gallishaw did not sign on for abroad when they signed on for six months duty.

I don't see why in the world she has chosen me, because there are N.F.L.D girls who came over here in Sep. and we did not come until Dec.

I think some of the English girls feel jealous; and I do not blame them at all: for I think matron or head quarters should have sent those instead of me who hasn't been here long. Of course they must keep on some senior V.A.Ds here, that is girls who have been here over a year; in fact, some have been two years.

After serving one year, you are entitled to a stripe to be worn on sleeves of dress and coat.

I haven't yet been on night duty: but our night nurse will soon be finished her night duty, and perhaps I shall take her place.

Gallishaw and Bartlett are going on night duty to-morrow night.

Three girls left for France to-day. Oh! we have so many things to get ready. I have not yet started to get anything, as we do not know where we shall be sent. If we go East, we have to get entirely different clothing from those required going West.

I went down town to-day and got ½ dozen handker-chiefs.

I am living in a state of wondering now; all we know is, that at any time we shall be notified to get ready for abroad.

I am writing this letter in the ward; everything is very quite, and everybody is very quiet. This is the first time I have ever had an opportunity to sit down in the ward, since I came here.

We have only about 20 patients now, and some of them are well enough to go to a concert in 2B.

Rosee is gone somewhere: but I don't know where. I miss him when he goes out; for he is a very mischievous boy. Just think, he is the one who has been here seventeen months; but it is so nice to see him able to get around on crutches.

The other morning I had to go across to 2B ward to deliver parcels that were sent by mistake to 3A ward. When I got back again, Rosee had great big coal cinders put in my clean water that I had ready to scrub lockers. He is always up to some mischief or other. Last night I was rolling bandages on the machine by his bed; he came along to fix his bed, and threw the blankets right over my head; when I was in the adjoining room the other morning, he tied me in; he is told quite often about his idleness; but poor boy, he must do something. Sometimes he says he is tired of everything, the hospital, the nurses and all.

(He is just coming in the ward door now. I shall not speak to him, for when once he is wound up,[1] he does not know what time to stop.)

We are not allowed to speak but little to the patients, and to tell the truth we scarcely have time to speak to ourselves sometimes, and especially after a convoy.

(Rosee is started "Well Nurse", and then started banging the back of my chair. I do hope Sister will give him a calling down.

He says he will tell me what to put down, he started "Dear Mother". I nearly died of laughing.)

One of the last convoy who came in, had a great piece taken out of his heel. It was blood poison caused by his boot rubbing his heel while marching. They have to do so many miles of marching, and then they had a running march.

Just imagine mother what that boy suffered when first he came to our ward: for of course his foot had to be put into a disinfectant bath before it was dressed or sponged. I really believe those boys are martyrs: for I am sure this boy must have undergone extreme agonies

---

1. A well-known Belleoram expression for high animation.

when putting his foot into the hot water. I am glad these foot baths are over for him. It is a miracle that it is getting better. He thought his foot would have to be amputated. This morning when I was bandaging it, he told me not to bandage it very tight over the wound: I know he must go through something when it is being dressed. After I was finished he said he was alright for another twenty four hours.

—

Sunday afternoon April 1st. (All fools' day).

This morning there was jolly fun among the patients. April 1st is kept exactly the same way as we do.[2]

I put a sheet of paper in an envelope and addressed it to Rosee; put a penny stamp on it. I gave it to the orderly to put in the mail bag. I should like to have been in the ward when the orderly opened the bag; for I know Rosee's expression would be something worth looking at. I was awfully sorry to miss the fun. I had asked the order-ly too, what time he would bring the mail and he said about 9:20 a.m.: it happened that was just our lunch hour in the duty room: however, he thought Sister did it: I don't believe for a minute that he thinks I did it.

It is bitterly cold in Lincoln to-day. It has been snow-ing nearly all day: but to tell the truth mother we have not had three inches of snow all the winter. The weather is damp here, a cold damp feeling, not the dry crisp air that

---

2. Two pages appear to be missing from original letter.

we have in N.F.L.D. Some mornings when we go to work, it is so disagreeable: perhaps before evening we have a very pleasant atmosphere. I always look out through the bedroom window when I get up to see what kind of day it is.

I tell you I stay in bed till the very last moment. I am afraid I shall be late some mornings now: for Gallishaw is moved to Queensway to live while on night duty; and Clare who occupies the room with me is a bit worse than I am myself. Gallishaw used to get up about ten minutes before I did; and soon as I see her with her pink petticoat on, then I knew it was time for me: but now I am at a loss. Of course I take my watch by the bed, and the maid knocks at 6:30; but her knocking affects me very little.

It isn't dark now when we go to the hospital; but quite light; of course it would be light now, so late in the spring.

I am awfully sorry to hear that your eye is bad again. How many times have we told you about things you would insist on doing. I hope when you write again that it will be better. Don't read so much mother by the lamp light. Why don't you ask McDermott[3] to see it, he may tell you what to do, and what not to do.

Good Bye Mother, take every care of yourself.

Your loving daughter Fanny.

---

3. Rev. Hugh MacDermott was a Congregationalist minister with some medical training located at Pool's Cove but travelling often to Belleoram.

Post Card
Charing Cross Station
London
April 27th 1917.
Friday morning.

To Mrs. Matilda Cluett
Belleoram, Newfoundland

Arrived here 4 a.m. on way to Boulogne. Had 2 hours delay in Sheffield. Four hours delay here. Going to Folkstone first. Ordered away in great haste. Pushed everything in trunk topsy-turvy. Travelling all night. Such experiences I never in all my life saw. Had breakfast 5:30 a.m. at Lyons, London. There are three of us. Henderson, Bridges and myself. Others are coming pretty soon.

Good Bye Mother.

I wish you could see us. I am wearing a grey summer uniform and black straw hat, badge on right breast. Red Cross on left arm.

Post Card
Charing Cross Station
April 27/17

To Miss Lily Cluett
Belleoram Newfoundland

Friday morning.

Dear Lil,

I just wrote a postal card to mother, I cannot say if she will get it or not.

We are now on the way to Folkstone. Cannot say what time we shall arrive in Boulogne.[1]

We are now having a cup of tea. It is ten minutes past eight am. This Station Hotel is marble all around. We have lots of luggage.

From Fan.

---

1. Boulogne–sur–Mer is located at the mouth of the river Liane on the French coast facing the Channel.

May 7th 1917
10 General Hos.
France.[1]

Dear Mother,

Did you receive the message I sent you when I arrived at [word missing].

I cannot tell you anything about the hospital here, as we must keep absolutely quiet on these matters in France.

[Word missing] is quite a large city and some parts of it are very pretty indeed.

Of course the hospital is not in the city; we have to take a car to get there.

I go for long walks in the morning, and make it an appointed time to get back to my tent by 12 a.m; at which time I go to bed.

I am on night duty, which accounts for my going to bed at noon.

I go on duty at ten minutes to eight in the evening and come off at 8 a.m. Night duty is no laughing matter especially if the wards are heavy.

I have the care of five wards at night; so you can imagine I am kept a bit busy. I sometimes feel very very sleepy around the hours of one and two; but sleep must

---

1. This is her first letter after transferring to the military hospital in Rouen, France. A number of words were removed from this letter by military censors for security purposes.

be sacrificed by all accounts, as one must keep a look out for all sorts of things, such as amputation bleedings, deaths, drinks etc.

This is a very wicked world mother: you cannot realize what sufferings there are: Some of the misery will ever live in my memory: it seems to me now as though I shall always have sad sights in my eyes.

I left my N.F.L.D friends in Lincoln. I miss them very, very much. Some of them were getting ready to go abroad somewhere; but I have not heard where. I don't expect to meet them this side of the Atlantic again.

I had a chance of going to [word missing] before coming here: it is quite hot enough here at times, I am sure I should absolutely melt there.

—

Wednesday evening

While waiting for breakfast at 7:15 p.m. I thought I would finish this letter.

I wrote a postal card to Susie and put it in an envelope addressed to you with the intentions of putting this letter in too: but dropped it in the box with the others by mistake.

I went for a walk this morning and completely lost my way. I went up by the horse depot and followed on and on until I thought it was time for me to turn tracks for home. Evidently, I turned a corner where I had no business to, the result was I found myself, heaven only knows where. By and by, I met a young girl and an old man in a wagon; I knew they were French, and it would be useless for one to stop them: but I did. I said "hospital" to her; she said "hopeetal" to me; Of course I knew then that she understood what I wanted: first, she hesitated for quite a while as to where it was; however, I had to turn around and go over same road I had already come; I walked on ahead of these people for quite a bit, then I hailed another French woman, who beckoned me to go into a building by the road side; she opened the door and called someone; it so happened that when I asked her if she could speak English, she said "Yes". I felt so glad I scarcely knew what to do; of course it was broken English; but even so, I understood from her that I had to go on the same direction I was going, then turn to the right; I went off at full speed knowing that it was drawing on for 12 a.m. my bed [time]. I still kept walking and walking; finally I stopped another French girl and said "hospital" to her. She marked a cross on her sleeve which meant "Red Cross Nurse"; I said "Yes" or "nodded" more likely. She chatted away in French as to the direction I was to go; but you know jolly well I didn't know a word she said. I at last nodded for her to come with me; poor girl! she walked until we came to a turning to the right, then left me with the understanding that I had to walk this road and turn to the right again. My word! I thought I would never get to a turning; but I did, and to get to the main road to take a train I had to walk through a "square", which is so large that it would take a considerable amount of time to walk from one end to the other: it was another such place as [word missing].

I told you I passed the horse Depot: it is called Horse

Convalescent Depot, where horses are brought from the lines to be treated. There were hundreds and hundreds and hundreds of horses on the grounds. I do wish some body else from Belleoram was here to see things: you cannot imagine what is going on in the world these war days: it is indeed very very wonderful.

I had to get lots of things for coming to France. My Kit bag cost £7.

There were in it a camp bed, mattress, rubber sheet, canvas wash stand, canvas bucket, camp chair, tent strap, candle lantern, small kettle.

I also had to get long rubbers, regulation trunk, hold all, roll up, small mirror, etc, etc, etc.

In my roll up is a knife and fork, table spoon, tea spoon, tin opener.

My "hold all" cost 14s 6d. It is made of waterproof with pockets on inside for holding things. It is something this shape.[2]

They hold quite a pile.

My regulation trunk was 27s; the trouble was it had to be no longer than 30 inches by 12 deep.

It was a nice one when I bought it; but you see it had to be taken from Lincoln to Sheffield, from there to Mary[le]bone; from there to Charing Cross London, from there to [word missing], from there to [word missing], from there to [word missing], from there to my tent.

I had another dress, gray linen, cost 5s. I bought it from Clare, too small for her, hence my getting it so cheap.

---

2. In the original letter, Fanny drew a sketch of her "hold all" detailing its shape and compartments.

My blacking "outfit" was 2s.6d. That is a paste brush, velvet polishing pad, a tin of paste fitted nicely into a tin box.

My regular macking[3] was 32s; rubber hat 4s; rubber boots 17s: I cannot for the life of me say what it costs each one to come to France; we were paid £33 to provide for the outfit which was more than good.

I must close now to get some sleep. I had a letter from Miss Elliot, St. John's, this morning; you heard me speak of her when I was at Seamen's Institute. Tell Bish to write. I'm sending Rhynie a postal card. Did you get the papers I sent from Lincoln with some knick knacks in them.

Good Bye Mother. I am writing this sitting up in my tent on the camp bed. I received your letter saying Bill Dicks was dead.

Your loving daughter Fannie.

Don't bother mother about sending a French dictionary. I have to get as much as I possibly can of another language. I guess you know which one.

---

3. Macintosh: a raincoat.

June 8, 1917, Rouen, France[1]

. . . building with beds in either side. No upstairs. Certainly a hut. They were cleaning 3B ward, and their patients were put in our ward. Oh mother! If you could only see some of the patients. Talk of the war. It is a crime. If only you people would glimpse some of the suffering ones: so many of them so young too. In our ward only, there are so many with two legs clean gone with just stumps of the thigh left. Some of them in spite of it all are quite cheery. Several times to day, they have struck up singing "Just break the news to mother". Oh my! there were two very distressed poor souls. One called to me to day to ask "Sister" for some cough medicine for him. It seemed as though he was suffering agonies, that to cough would nearly kill him. I shall never forget his face. When Sister and Nurse were dressing one for the night; "oh sister"! He used to say so often; I know he was in an awful state; I could not stay to see his wounds, as I had to get a clean sheet from "Duty Room", and tidy wards for the nights. I was off duty yesterday morning from 9 am until 12. We have breakfast at 6:30 am; a light luncheon around 9 am, Dinner at 1 p.m., tea at 4:30 pm, supper at 7 p.m, but if we get off duty at 5 pm, we do not bother to go back to the Hospital for supper.

---

1. The beginning portion of this letter is missing.

We have to be back to the Hostel by 9:30 for the night. The first thing I have to do from 7 am until 9 o'clock is to scrub two long ward tables, 8 long benches, 2 small tables, dust the centre of the ward, that means dust two pianos and a few other things, and then from time on until lights are out which is at 8 o'clock, there is washing and bathing the patients, their meals etc. I never know when I am going to be sent to wash a patient, and the poor things are very miserable sometimes; but on the whole it is wonderful to see how happy they are under some awful circumstances.

—

Friday night: 8th

I have got my second day over. I had to help sister with some dressings to day. Oh mother! I shall never forget it as long as I live. There was one man wounded in the thigh: there was a hole right through from side to side. It was like you cut it with an axe. The sister used to put dressing right through the hole, and put a rubber tube right through the hole and syringe it. Such sights one will never forget. You can read about war, and the wounded, but when you are brought face to face with it, I tell you, it is heart rending.

We are spring cleaning, that is our ward which is 3A, had to be taken into 3B. It took six of us to lift one man out of bed. Three stretcher bearers, two Sisters and myself got him out. To night our ward will be disinfected ready for the Charwomen to morrow morning.

One boy from 3B ward came into our ward yesterday evening and played comic songs, they nearly all, in spite of their wounds struck up singing. One boy played a mouthorgan. Some of them are so funny. The Scotch boys talk different to the English: I have to ask them over so many times.

This seems to be quite a place for Zeppelins. As soon as we hear "Buzzer", we have all to assemble in sitting room: that is the time then. The second last "Zepp" dropped bombs, and injured the ground a bit. They have made a new rule here now. I just heard it tonight. The nurses are going to be ask[ed] if they will sign for as long as they will be wanted.

If I get a couple of days off I am going to take a trip to Scotland. I am acquainted with Nurse Davison from Edinburgh, and I shall go with her. There are nurses here from Canada and all parts of the globe. We have one nurse who was an operator at Cairo. I cannot write anymore to night mother.

Good Bye.

From your daughter Fannie.

Frances Cluett, centre, at her graduation of Normal training school 1901. (Photo courtesy of Mary Cluett.)

Frances Cluett, VAD

Frances Cluett, top left, among her students. Also in photograph are: Waldron Cluett (bottom left-hand corner), Edward Cluett (right of Waldron Cluett), and Arthur Cluett (two right of Frances Cluett, with three girls in white behind him). Arthur is the father of Ruby Cluett Korcurko, Edward is the brother of Arthur. Waldron is first cousin to Arthur and Edward. Arthur and Edward are the sons of Stephen Vatcher Cluett, who skippered the *Reya M. Cluett*. Fourth from right in back row is Bill Rompkey's father, William H. Rompkey, Sr. *c.* 1913. (Photo courtesy of Ruby Cluett Kocurko.)

Your Daughter Fanny

"Sister: Lillian. Mother: Matilda Cluett."

"Frances, grandfather, and Abisha Cluett."

"Belleoram. Susie enjoying the top of the Cluett Wood. Our fish store is the building."

"Cluett Wharf."

A VAD recruitment poster. (Photo couresty of Dr. David Parsons.)

Frances Cluett in her VAD uniform.

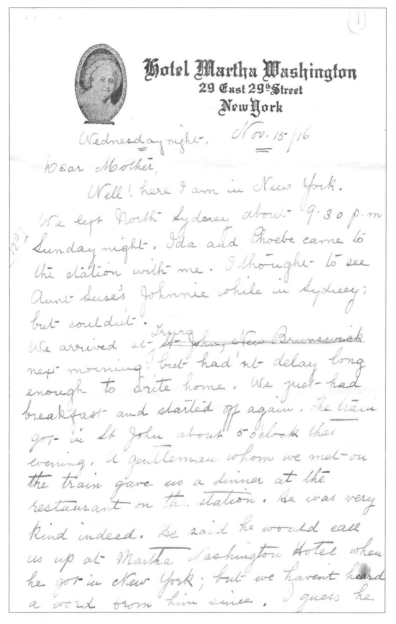

The first page from of one of Fanny's letters dated November 15, 1916, from Hotel Martha Washington, New York.

Frances Cluett, VAD

VAD nurses (L–R): Henrietta Gallishaw (1891–1945), St. John's;
Frances Cluett (1883–1969), Belleoram (front); Bertha Bartlett
(1896–1918), Brigus; and Clare Janes (1897–1948), Hant's
Harbour.

Mrs. Adeline Elizabeth Browning, C.B.E.
(Photo taken from *Newfoundland Quarterly.*)

"Battle area. Sister Hart. Cambrai / Peronne on road sign."

Cluett family history recounts that this German Iron Cross
medal was given to Fanny by a dying German soldier.

Frances Cluett and Billy Williams.

"Miss Newton from Cornwall. She was my friend. We shared
same hut in France."

No. 21 Base Depot medical store, Rouen, France.

"Dear Paddy who would not go to sleep until I brought him a
cup of tea in his hospital bed."

"During the War. Roland Ashford [centre], a very nice boy indeed, writes very amusing letters."

"Ruins, April 1919." France.

"London July 1919. House members at VAD hostel Ecclestone Square. We stayed there many days waiting for orders to go to Turkey."

"Summer 1920 Constantinople. Mrs. Morton enjoying situation with Lieutenant Dutton. Billy Williams [right] looking on."

War Office,

Adastral House,

Victoria Embankment,

E.C. 4, .

83/6638·

11. 8· 1919.

Madam,

I beg to inform you that your present ongagement with the Nursing Staff of the Army terminated on 24. 6. 19.   .

A further communication will be addressed to you regarding your pay and allowances, which will cease from the date given.

    I am,

        Madam,

        Your obedient Servant,

Miss F. Cluett
V.A.D Hostel
74 Ecclston Sq.
Victoria
S.W.

        Matron-in-Chief,
        Q.A.I.M.N.S.

Fanny's discharge papers.

"Homecoming arch."

10th Gen. Hospital,
B.E.F
Rouen, France.
Aug.25/17

Saturday Night.

Dear Mother,

I received your letter night before last: my letters from home are few and far between.

Did Rhynie get the one I wrote her a while ago? Tell Bish to write me; she hasn't written me a line for ages; surely she can spare a few minutes, if only to write a postal.

I sent some postals the other day addressed to Lil: I trust she will get them.

I am enclosing you a slip of my rose-tree:[1] the old leaves have dropped off it; I do wonder if the enclosed piece will root: it is very doubtful. I do wish you had seen it at first; it was gorgeous. I am sure mother you would have gone in ecstasies over it.

I have now in my own bedroom the most beautiful bunch of sweet peas you ever saw; such a variety of odours. Sister gave them to me; she got them at Colonel Monteith's garden; he has them in profusion; I met him

---

1. Fanny always kept a garden; in Belleoram her flowers regularly decorated the church and even in the midst of war, such is her strength of spirit, her optimism, her hope, she insists on cultivating beautiful flowers.

on the train the other day, and he told me to come to his garden one evening and get some; but I haven't gone yet; I must certainly go very soon; or they will be dropping; judging from what I hear; his garden must be a picture.

Mother I have never seen as many flowers in all my life as I have seen since I came to Rouen. All the hospital tents have them at their front entrances; oh! they are beautiful.

On my way to my ward; I pass beds and beds of red and pink geraniums, assorted asters, assorted daisies, beds edged with pansies, and flowers that we do not grow in Belleoram.

Last Sunday I went into Rouen, and took a walk in the country which is a bit up hill; I looked around me; the sur-roundings were exactly as I have seen them in books. One could never believe there was such exquisite scenery in the world.

On my way home this evening in the train, I was talk-ing to a sergeant who in civil days was in some kind of Academy he of course started talking about sketching and so forth; he by and by said he was at 29 I.B.D. (Twenty Nine Infantry Base Depot) that is where the N.F.L.D. boys are, or at least some of them; however he was telling me about our boys; he likes them very much indeed as they stick up for each other etc; but they had little discipline. I have heard several times that the N.F.L.D. boys are hard to govern.

Well! on arriving at our camp, whom should I meet when I got off the train - Tib Poole.[2] His attention was called to me by the above sergeant, who said "here is a

---

2. Stephen Poole, from Belleoram.

N.F.L.D boy;" I turned behind and came face to face with Tib. Imagine my surprise.

He is looking very well indeed, seems to be grown taller: and looks extremely smart in khaki.

He told me that Freeman Fudge[3] will soon be coming over; so I shall try to see him also.

Oh yes! I saw Charlie Carter[4] and Big Pat Burke's son Leonard[5] last week. I knew they had arrived in Rouen and were at 29 I.B.D. Sergt. Janes informed me of their whereabouts: so as soon as I received Sergt's letter, I immediately set off for their depot. After walking and walking and seeing no one with a shoulder badge of N.F.L.D, I made tracks for our camp again. Finally I heard footsteps behind me, then my attention was called. I turned back and saw two faces; I did not know them only that they were N.F.L.Ders; but one was Leonard Burke, the other was from Torbay. I enquired after Charlie Carter and George Dicks; was told George had left but Charlie was about the depot somewhere. Leonard Burke kindly went and fetched him for me. Oh! Charlie has grown so big, and looks years older. Of course he is Corporal now, and is addressed by the privates as Corporal; he wears two stripes; He is much more of a man than when he left Belleoram; of course he has some

---

3. Also from Belleoram.
4. Charles Fred Carter from Belleoram. He was awarded the Distinuished Conduct Medal during the Battle of Ledegham, October, 1918. The citation says: "He worked his way forward with his section through a timber yard to outflank an enemy machine-gun which was assailing the Newfoundland line. From his advanced position his fire silenced the offending German gun and continued to harass the enemy during the entire counterattack."
5. Leonard Patrick Burke of St. John's. The Burkes were a prominent family in St. Jacques.

responsibility now; he told me he had to go before the Colonel in the morning. I think the Colonel saw a man who wasn't in his place, and of course it was up to Charlie to see that he was. I promised I would drop him a line.

I had a letter from Vince a long while ago, and answered it. I have been waiting nearly two weeks for an answer; I must drop him a postal; he may not have got the letter.

To day in the ward, one of the patients told me he belonged to the Division where the NFLD boys are; but he was an Englishman I think. I asked him if he by chance had ever met a Cluett up the line; he said "Do you mean Officer Cluett?: I said "Yes", he replied, "I have waited on him" and that he was a "nice young fellow". The world is small after all.

I cannot write any more mother. Excuse lead pencil. My fountain pen leaks, and in addition to that I upset a bottle of ink on my sheet. I always write in bed.

To morrow I have to write Gallishaw, Janes and several others. Janes has moved nearer the fighting line.

I am glad to know mother you are keeping well. I should loved to have been able to go bake apple picking with you and Lil. I can imagine you going through the tuck-a-moors[6] over to Big Pond.[7]

Good Night Mother.

From Your daughter Fannie.

---

6. Small trees or shrubs.
7. Quite a large pond about forty fathoms deep back of Belleoram where boys and girls fished in summer and skated in winter.

France
Rouen.
B.E.F.
10 Gen. Hos.

Thursday Night.
Sept.13/17

Dear Mother,

You will see I am sending you a present. Send it to St John's and get it cashed; I drew it on the Bank of Commerce, St John's.

You will have no difficulty in getting it cashed. Johnny or Levi Angus[1] will explain to you; I send it this way, because it is the safest; for if the draft is lost, I can easily refer to Cox's Bank at Rouen. I trust you will get it alright.

I got the cake parcel; but sad to say the cakes were mixed together as one and beaten to pieces just like sawdust: First looking into the box you would really think it was a box of sawdust; but of course it tasted quite differently; I am more than thankful to you mother for sending them; it was a great pity they were smashed; it is very little use sending an a cardboard box; it is bound to get broken. I would rather you did not send any more mother, much as I value them; for I do not get the bene-

---

1. McCuish, the Customs Officer in Belleoram.

fit of them; it was five weeks coming: the candy was in good condition.

Oh Yes! the very first thing I saw, was one piece of the money lying on the crumbs, so that will give you an idea of how it was banged about.

I took one piece of the chocolate to the ward and part-ed it between some of my patients: I should not give any of the cake away unless I gave it in a tablespoon.

I was so glad of the sugar, for one cannot buy an ounce for love or money. I have a tin of cocoa in my room that one of the patients gave me, and almost every night before I go to bed I have a cup of it; but without sweet-ness; so mother that sugar is like gold to me; one has almost to count the grains before using it. I don't think I shall make a cup to night, as it is rather late, and our lights have to be out at 10.30 p.m; but I have a candle though.[2]

—

Dear Mother,[3]

The first part of this letter was posted this afternoon; I did not care to put the whole letter in with the cheque as the letter had to be censored in Rouen instead of the camp; and of course when you are standing by the officer cen-soring them; you are jolly glad to have just a little bit of writing; it is not the same when we get them censored in

---

2. The letter abruptly ends here.
3. This letter was originally attached to the first, however Fanny ulti-mately decided it was best to mail them separately.

our camp; for we just drop the letters in opened into the letter box and know nothing more about them.

Good Bye Mother,

I daresay you will get this letter and the first part at the same time: you will write and let me know right away won't you mother?

The enclosed[4] is one of the many coloured asters all around the hospital: they are much larger than that one.

---

4. The original letter contained an aster: a purple flower which blooms in fall.

Rouen
B.E.F. France
28-9-17

Friday 8. a.m.

Dear Lil,

You will wonder what on earth I am doing to write you at this hour of the morning.

I am having the day off: we have a whole day a month and half a day a week; but we do not get a half day in the week that we have taken the whole day.

However; I have just this minute finished my breakfast sitting up in bed. One of the V.A.Ds working in the mess brought it to my room; it consisted of white bread and butter - I mention white bread because we never get it in the mornings; evidently there is an exception made on your day off — and a tea-pot of tea, about an ounce of sugar, raspberry jam, a sausage and a wee bit of fried bread which is always so hard that I never eat it: but some of the girls think its excellent: I drank the whole teapot of tea, ate all the bread, left nothing except a bit of butter and the fried bread.

Nurse Donald and I are going down the river to La Bouille:[1] we must be in Rouen by 10 am for the boat; so I can lie back a little while longer yet; there is no need of

---

1. La Bouille is approximately eighteen kilometres northwest of Rouen.

telling you what I shall wear as it will be only strictly uniform; a coat with the red cross on left arm, badge over right breast; numerals on shoulder straps, NFLD emblem on collar; badge in front of hat; white gloves, black hat, white silk waist with black tie, black glazed belt, black serge skirt. We leave Rouen at 10 am, get back at 6 p.m; I think we shall walk back to view the surroundings, although it is a terribly long journey.

I heard there was a convoy in last night; thank goodness, I am escaping it for once; to think I shall have no beds to make or washings to give out, or foments to make, or medicines to give, or lockers to tidy, or kits to tie up etc etc etc for one whole day.

—

6.45 pm.

We have just returned from La Bouille, and I have tidied myself a bit for 7.15 dinner; we were covered with dust as we walked all the way back, a distance of about 10 1/4 miles or 18 kilometres as we call it in France; quite a walk wasn't it: we arrived at La Bouille somewhere near 12 am; went up to the top of the hill to the "Hotel in the woods" and had a dinner which cost us four francs each: but that was not at all expensive. Here is what we had. First course, bread and butter and cider, then we had omelette, then fried mushroom and potatoes, then cheese and grapes: oh! I forgot to say we had melon for first course. You are not asked what you will have but the things are brought in whether you like them or not. The

Hotel was very nice inside, quite plain; but solid and good looking; the walls were fawn coloured, beautiful red carpet, no pictures or anything about; it was very nice room indeed.

Donald and I were the only occupants for a few minutes; but people, a man and a girl stepped off an automobile and came in. They were very amusing. I wish poor Ernest John had been with me; you see I was facing them and could take it all in; but Donald was back on; but anyhow she would not have seen the humourous side: for she is so staid in everything, and yet so young.

The two in question were acting as much: I shall never forget them. They walked across the Hotel, into the hall as tho' they owned France. He sat our side of the table and she the other; talking French of course; whether they understood English or not I don't know: I am inclined to think the man did; for once I said to Donald, "I should like to live here," the man immediately looked across at me.

The girl had black hair and wore it on the sides like this.[2] Every once in a while he would put her hand up and flatten it on the face. He started in to stroke his eyebrows and twist his moustache: it was screamingly funny.

We left there at 2:15 pm for Rouen: oh! it was such a lovely day: we found our way along by the sign boards with hands pointing the required direction, otherwise we should never have found the right road, for they were branching off in every direction, not one straight road

---

2. In the original letter, Fanny drew a sketch of the hairstyle.

like going down the Gull Point;[3] I do wish you could take a peep at some of the surroundings about Rouen: they are very very beautiful.

—

Oct. 3rd Wednesday night.

You must think I am never going to finish this letter; I think myself I am a very long time about it.

I haven't yet finished about my day off. Well! after dinner at 7.15 p.m on my "day off"; I walked ever so far to a cinema at the Boy Scouts. I wasn't a bit tired, neither was I next day; but Donald did not go to the cinema.

I have indeed been enjoying good health since I came to Rouen, much better than in England, for there I had a cough all the time, and was cured instantly I may say after I came here.

The only thing I feel is my back; of course it is from bed making. I start making beds at 7.30 and finish about 9.15 or thereabouts; we don't stop between the beds, but one constant rush, just as fast as the hand can go. The beds in F9 are very very low; a little lower and I should have to kneel on the floor to make them: you can imagine how hard that is on the back.

This morning in F9, we never had one up patient to help me; I had to go to another of my wards F12 and get a patient from there to help me a while. Of course I could

---

3. A turn or point on the main road through Belleoram leading to the end of the community and on down to the Barachois or "Barsway" in those days.

not keep him long as he is a patient even if he does get up.

This afternoon I was on alone: it was Sister's turn off duty from 5-8. I had lots of washings to give out: but thank goodness they are able to wash themselves.

For every drop of boiling water I use for inhalations etc. I have to go to the cook house across the way for it.

I assure you we haven't every convenience in these medical tents.

I had to bathe the eyes of 5 men who were gassed, and that takes a bit of time; I then had to give 4 inhalations of boiling water and Friars balsam for gassed throats; I had to put a Perchloride dressing of gauze and wool on a man's thigh; and had to powder a gassed burnt back which was simply awful. There were temp. and pulses in F4 and F9 and F12 to take; but I could not get through with them all; I took 37 and booked and charted them, the others I left for Sister when she came on at 5 pm.

This morning there was so much work to be got through in F9, that one scarcely knew when and where to begin. There was no patient orderly to help the R.A.M.C.[4]

---

4. The Royal Army Medical Corps was, and is, a pillar of army medical services in the British Army. During WWI both experienced and inexperienced men joined the RAMC. Wounded men were removed from the battlefield by infantry soldiers acting as stretcher-bearers and brought back to the Regimental Aid Post. After RAP treatment the RAMC took over, evacuating the wounded behind the front lines. Afterwards, more serious cases were transported to a Casualty Clearing Station by ambulance, while others hitched rides or, if they could, walked to the CCS. The CCS was a field hospital where the badly hurt were immediately treated and where major surgery was performed. Then, by road or ambulance train, patients were taken to England or to the base hospitals near the coast such as Fanny's hospital at Rouen. There they were treated and either sent back to their units or discharged as invalids by a board of RAMC doctors.

orderly; he of course had to clean breakfast dishes for 26 men, and take the laundry away after I had it changed: however I swept the ward for him; it was a sweep I assure you, under 24 beds, and you know it is white floor, and some of the boards are very rough, the dust would insist on sticking into it which meant additional labour.

The band is now playing, another draft going up the line; to watch the thousands of them sends the cold creeps all over one.

They sing out "Good Bye," "Good Night" etc; they appear to be awfully jolly: out of the thousands very few return.

You told me before I left I should never stand the work. I remember hearing you say about staying in the ward with the dead. Ah! Lil, many a bedside have I stood by and watched the last breath; with the rats rushing underneath the bed in groups; and the lights darkened. I do not dwell on some of the horrible and terrible sights I have witnessed, for my first night duty was in the German Compound amidst the most pitiful surroundings that anybody on earth could imagine. I never said before that I had been nursing Germans, but I was with them two months on night duty. I had five or six tents to look after. I was the only V.A.D on then. Of course there was a sister to come through occasionally.

I could never make you sensible of the sights I have seen; I got a squashed finger one night.

The German orderly was helping me to move a bed with a helpless patient in it. The foot of the bed came down; he picked it up too quickly for me, squashing the nail. My finger came between the iron bars; it is better now though.

I must close now: I've got so many to write. Good night. I got Rhynie's letter to night. Give my love to mother. Tell Bish to write.

From Fan.

Rouen
10 Gen Hos.
26-10-17

Dear Mother,

This is Friday night. I did not get off duty time enough for dinner. I had to wait for the night nurses to come on which is at 8 pm; but one of them which does my wards did not get in until 8.30 pm; dinner is not served after 8.20 pm.

We have one very sick person, gassed terribly; he has oxygen turned on him every hour for 5 minutes; every 4 hrs he has to have gas mixture medicine: then his throat has to be sprayed; he has been awfully miserable this afternoon and evening; the perspiration would pour off him when trying to breathe; I hate to think of him lying there tonight suffering agonies; he has been calling to us every minute to sit with him. He used to say "I am frightened"; every time I passed through the ward, I had to go and sit with him; he could scarcely speak when I came off at 8.30; poor chap! I wonder if he will live until mid night. All his back and one side of his face and a part of his thigh are burnt. You haven't any idea mother what he is suffering: he was put on the D.I list (Dangerously ill) this evening. His eyes were shut for three days when first he came in: he could not see or speak. It is really too terrible to think about. Oh! the difficulty I have had to get through the work this afternoon. I had three wards to attend to. Sister was having a half day off; one thing specially I had to report another gas blistered man to the Medical Officer to night; and I quite forgot all about it. He came through the ward too; I had to tell him about the very sick one and a few others. Sister will be mad in the morning because I said nothing about it. However, there it is.

Nearly all the patients we have got lately on the Medical Lines are gassed; that means their eyes have to be bathed and inhalations of boiling water and Friars balsam; a teaspoonful of balsam to a pint of boiling water. Many of them are burned but not blistered: that is with mustard gas; we do the burns with Baking Soda and Boracic Powders which heal them very quickly.

Sometimes I relieve on the Surgical Lines: It is there the horrible sights are; you would not believe me mother if I tell you about what I have seen and gone through. I always think of what Lil told me about not being able to stay in a ward with the dead. Tell her, I have stood by many a bed side in the middle of the night, with lights darkened, watching for the last breath, then put screens about him, and in addition to that, the rats would rush underneath the beds with a swish. I do not think about them mother; but I shall never forget some of the most piteous sights that ever could possibly be.

I don't think I ever told you I did night duty in the German Compound for Prisoners of War. I had five German wards to look after, and one of the wards was an acute surgical, where amputated legs and arms had to be watched for hemorrhages.

I think had you known that was where I was doing night duty you would have felt a bit uneasy. Of course there was an English night orderly also. It was funny, I did not feel at all scared; but perhaps I did feel a bit nervous sometimes.

I knew they would not harm me there, or at least I suppose they couldn't: I have passed through their wards with them lying on either side; sometimes I used to think, if they would only jump up; but then on the whole I had nothing whatever to complain about; they were always very respectful to me. The Colonel came to me one night and asked me if I had any complaints to make against them; I could speak quite a bit of German while I was there; but I have forgotten most of it now, not having reason to speak it. I could tell you heaps of things but I daren't. One night in the German Compound I was stopped by the English Sentry outside the barbed wire who wanted to know about one of the German orderlies; he said he was carrying a light in his hand which he would revolve at intervals: of course, I knew nothing about it; but had to go through the wards and inquire if either one of them had been using an electric torch; but they hadn't; I think it must have been a cigarette that security saw; being a VAD is not all sunshine mother.

We were awakened the other night by the air raid. Oh the awful noise of the guns.

I used to stand by the barbed wire Compound when I was on night duty and listen to the guns on the battlefield. About 2 p.m they would be at their loudest. We always know after a rush at the front that our wards will soon be full again.

—

Sat. 8 pm.

The patient I was telling you about that was so badly gassed died at 1.30 pm last night: I knew he was dead before I went for duty this morning: for mother I thought he called me during the night – however I woke up, and of course when I went on duty, the first thing I saw was the empty bed: poor chap - he suffered terribly; out of all we did for him, we could not save him.

I have had a half-day today. Nurse Taylor and I went into town about 2 pm and got home again at 7 pm, We walked into Rouen which is quite a nice long walk: We then went to the jewellers to get my watch, I took it there to get a glass put on it: afterwards we went to Cox's Bank to change a cheque for Taylor, but alas! they had closed. I think it is closed on Saturday afternoons, or from mid-day on.

We next went to a shop to get a sketch book, then after trying a considerable length of time for a pair of nail scissors, which we could not get without taking the manicure set; we suggested that we had better try another place which we did without success.

Taylor wanted to get a transfer for her tea cloth, but we could not get it in any shop.

Then we went to a tea room and had something to eat. I had café au lait! Taylor had black coffee. We dawdled about from one place to another until it was time to come home, which meant another long walk. Of course we could have taken the train; but we just loved to walk, the night was so beautiful.

On our way to Rouen, we went into the Public Gardens. Oh mother it is a place worth visiting: I am going to send you some slips shortly of the most beautiful chrysanthemums you ever saw.

I cannot write anymore tonight mother.

Good Bye. Tell Bish to write.

I am writing Susie shortly.

Your loving daughter Fannie.

Dear Mother,

I felt as though I couldn't close the envelope without dropping a line to you.

Have you been well this fall: I am quite well now: but had an awful cold; apart from that I never felt better in my life.

I sent a card to Art the other day; I hope he will answer it.

Did you get the present I sent you a while ago; will send another shortly.

I shan't write much mother: for I am dreadfully sleepy; I think I get all your letters; however I've got the cakes, and mean to have a bit before I go to bed.

I am still in same wards that I was put in when I came off night duty; but am expecting a change every day.

We do not see the horrible sight in the Medical Lines as on the Surgical Lines; we had one poor chap tried to commit suicide one night. I knew he was not too well; for I called the M.O.'s attention and the Asst. Matron's to him before I came of[f] duty; I also told the other boys to have an eye on him. When I went on duty in the morning. I saw an empty bed and knew what had happened without asking; shortly after that our night orderly had to be sent to a mental ward.

One of our patients who was not able to move in bed, as his kidneys were gone, would have given me a fright, but for the orderly. The orderly told me that when he came in one end door of the ward, this poor boy was going out the other end; of course he was dying; and died next morning while I stood by his bed; he was about seventeen or eighteen. However badly the surgical boys are wounded, they seem quite merry and cheerful, and can enjoy a laugh well as anyone. I think the majority of them pull through; for they are well attended.

The 10 General[1] is giving a concert at Xmas. I enjoy them more now than I ever did. I went with Sister Drabble one night and laughed until the tears rolled from my eyes. She is so funny and humourous. I must get to bed. I expect we shall have another convoy to night; as 12 divisions went over the top yesterday.

Good night mother.

Write soon.

From Fannie.

Enclosed are postal cards of damage done by German air raids. Our orderly gave them to me.[2]

---

1. No. 10 General is the name of the hospital.
2. Included with the original letter, there were numerous postcards, each with varying amounts of damage including burn marks and charred remnants.

Rouen.
10 Gen. Hos.
9-12-17
[December 9, 1917]
Sunday night.

Dear Mother,

It seems quite a long time since I have written you; my letters from home are few and far between. Have you yet received the cheque I sent you; it is weeks and weeks ago; every day I think I shall hear from you, saying you received it; do please write when and let me know, so that I make enquiries if it be lost.

Isn't it awfully sad about Vincent:[1] I am waiting word from Etaples,[2] then I shall write Aunt Sarah. I am sure she thinks very hard of it: but what a joy to know he is buried and not lying on the open battle fields. I wrote him: but received no answer, finally I heard he was wounded; then I received the cablegram from Ray; but could not wire

---

1. Lieutenant Vincent Cluett was wounded in fighting at Masnières on November 21, 1917, and died five days later in hospital.
2. Located on the northern French coast, Etaples was a small town of about 5,000 known chiefly as a small fishing and commercial port. It became a huge Allied military camp and then the site of a large hospital complex where injured soldiers were treated before they returned to the Front or to the United Kingdom. Because of its importance as a medical centre, it was the target of many German air raids, including four incendiary bomb attacks in May 1918.

him, as I was not supposed to know it until after 4 days, but then I knew they would be officially notified before that time. Last Saturday night I was at N.F.L.D. head quarters in Rouen, making inquiries about him; Sergt. Dewling from St John's told me that his people would probably hear of his death on Monday night; and did they hear on Monday night mother.

He used to write me such long letters describing everything, and of course I used to write some very funny things to him; but never again.

The N.F.L.D. regiment is getting served pretty badly: in the last attack nearly all the officers were killed. While I was talking to Sergt. Dewling, the phone rang, which told him of more deaths of our boys. He says our boys are getting cut up altogether; he cannot think how the ranks are going to be filled again; yet they are still coming; as seventy are now on their way.

The boys who come down the line now, say that the war is worse than at Dardanelles: oh! mother, if you could only see and hear all we do; I assure you it is not very nice, when you have to rip the khaki off them in bed; blood everywhere; and then to hear them tell what they have gone through; it is very sad to see troops marching daily to take the trains for the line; bands playing: yet they seem so cheerful; and call Good Bye to us who watch them over the camp fences.

To night I went to Con Camp to Church. I love to go there: the orchestra is splendid. I was off duty last Sunday night, and off this Sunday night. The sermons for this Sundays refer to the minister and his Calling; very, very interesting. I should love to go next Sunday; but I don't expect to be off duty. The collection tonight was towards getting a few more musical instruments; a bass clarinet.

We sang, "Hark, hark my soul", and "Thou whose Almighty Word". The minister is a splendid speaker: he gave an account of how he first started to become a minister.

Well! after I came back from Church, I found out that there had been two N.F.L.D boys to see me. They left their names; but I do not know either of them; they are calling again tomorrow night.

I went to see a N.F.L.D boy in C1 ward the other day: he is a Forsey[3] from Grand Bank, a cousin of Blanche Forsey's.

I am moved from my old wards, and put in the surgical side where they have crushed fingers, boils on the neck, bad toes, shrapnel grazings, synovitis knees,[4] etc; its nothing but foments all day.

Last night I went into town; but had an accident; I had just bought an ornament of a little boy whistling, a lovely thing, with his head thrown back, hands in the pockets, etc. I was knocked down by a horse coming round the corner, of course I wasn't hurt badly; but it shook me up a little. It's a miracle I escaped with no broken bones; the horse stopped immediately I was down; my pocket-book came open, sending things flying everywhere. The red-caps military police came to me and asked whose fault it was; but I wished to say nothing about it: In less than 5 minutes I

---

3. Claude Forsey.
4. When fluid accumulates around the capsule of the knee, the joint is swollen, painful, and tender, and motion is restricted.

couldn't see through the crowd of "Townies": I walked away, leaving them all there; I was so sorry when I found my ornament was broken.

What kind of weather are you having in Belleoram mother? We are having fairly good as yet.

My leave has been due since last of October. We are allowed to go to Paris now if we wish. Tell Lil I am sending her a pair of Wellington boots. They were a very good price. I do hope she will wear them; perhaps I shall send two pairs.

It is getting late. I have my laundry to pack up. Good night mother. Write soon. How is Win now?

From your daughter Fannie.

Rouen,
B.E.F.
Dec.29-12-17

Sunday night

Dear Mother,

Xmas is over; but I do wish you all a Merry one and a Happy New Year: but I suppose it is a bit difficult to be joyous under present circumstances; still these are things one must cope with daily: I can imagine poor Aunt Sarah and Uncle Walt; I cannot yet realize Vince is dead: I did think we were going to meet some day in France; I even went so far as to think he would be getting "leave" somewhere about my time then we should spend it together.

I received a letter written by him before he was wounded; but it did not reach me until days after his death: it gave me a weird feeling to read that letter, knowing the writer had passed away; but I shall visit the grave before leaving France; it isn't far from Boulogne.

I received two boxes from home. Will you thank the senders mother? for I cannot write them all, although I may drop each one a postal.

The cake wasn't hashed at all this time, but a bit dried. The tea Aunt Emily sent me, I took it to the ward on Xmas Day to make tea for Nurse Parker, Owen-Davies, Wilcox and Sister Lucas. We had our tea together on the ward table; but it was so draughty all around, that the tea party was nearly a failure.

I went into town a few days before Xmas with "Sister" to purchase cakes, etc, for the boys' tea on Xmas day. We went to the E.F.C Expedition Force Canteen for there things are ever so much cheaper than elsewhere: the French charge us abominably for everything.

However, we bought tinned damsons, dried prunes, potted salmon, potted meat, nuts, apples, cake etc. With the cake we made "trifle"; that is, you put the cake in slices on the bottom of a bowl or pan, then a layer of fruit. then custard or jelly or Blanc Mange; it is very good. Sister made the "trifles" for her four wards.

Out of the fruit we made fruit salad: that is we put all the different kinds of fruit we had into one bowl: of course there was a lot of syrup with them as we had tinned fruit to mix with it. Three of our wards did their fruit that way: but I didn't, for one of my up patients told me it would be much better to keep the fruit separately; as some of the patients may not like all the different kinds of fruit.

This up patient was such a help to me in decorating the wards; he helped me with one half of the ward, and practically did the second half all by himself: he was a splendid decorator; he has done quite a bit of work in that line pre war days.

Matron gave us some coloured paper decorations; but not enough; so with some tissue paper we made some ourselves, and hung in festoons from the ceiling of the tents; of course we had no hammering to do, for we could easily pin through the canvas.

(I must put this letter up, for one of the nurses has a talking ticket; she has not ceased talking a minute for the past couple of hours); however I am having a day off to-morrow: oh! mother won't it be ripping to stay in bed; I shall have my breakfast brought to the cubicle. Good night mother.

—

Monday 30-17. [December 30, 1917]

It is now 9 p.m. I have had my day off. I stayed in bed until 12 a.m: got up and dressed for lunch, after which I tidied my room, as I was absolutely ashamed of it, then at 3 pm I went into Rouen to get some knitting needles; I have started to knit myself a pair of stockings, I expect to finish them about June.

I am preparing for my leave: I don't know where I shall go until I hear from Clare who is at St Omer.[1] She wrote me saying her leave would be due in a month's time, so I shall wait for her. I have suggested that we should go to the South of France. "Sister", who has just come back, is in ecstasy over it, and strongly [urged] me to go there. I have also written Gallishaw about our leave, as I know hers will be due very soon. I think she is going home in January. Poor old Gallishaw, I would give worlds to see her.

I shall not write any more tonight mother. My knitting

---

1. St. Omer in Norde Pas-de-Calais, is north of Rouen, approximately twenty-seven miles inland from Calais.

is waiting; and I am just longing to get at it. "A new broom sweeps clean".

Good night,

Give my love to Aunt Suse.

From Fannie.

10 Gen. Hos.
Rouen
4-2-18
[February 4, 1918]

Sunday night

Dear Mother,

It is now about 5 minutes past ten. I have just got into bed, and am scribbling this lying down. I wish you could take a peep into my cubicle. I have a candle lit on the chair, and a small oil-stove lit, to warm water on to wash myself before going to sleep: this oil stove is very small, yet it heats the room splendidly. Almost every-body has one in her cubicle.

I usually wash my face and hands at night; so in the morning I can just show my face to the water. Needless to say, I have very little time for any thing else, as many a time, the 7 o'clock breakfast bell rings, and I am lying quite comfortably in bed. You can imagine mother, how I get out with a hop, skip and a jump. I dress in ten minutes; but you see I have only twenty minutes for my breakfast; not that, to be punctual, for I am supposed to be on my wards at 7:30 am; my bed has to be made before 7:30 too. I tell you mother, we do not let the grass grow under our feet.

Oh Mother! I am so sleepy in the mornings. When I get home, I shall have to stay in bed until dinner-time for a week.

I am still in G3 Ward, kept rather busy, but nothing heavy. You see it is a local ward, therefore the patients are slightly hurt: Convoy patients direct from the front line, of course are exceedingly heavy, such as amputated legs, and arms; gun shot wounds in the head, and all over the body practically: most horrible sights.

I do G3 myself: but of course if Sister Lucas is about, she does the rounds with the MO (Medical Officer): but if she chanced to be out to Matron's office or 9:30 lunch; it falls to me to go through the ward with him.

It is very laughable some times, for the M.O. orders things I never heard of before; so I wonder to myself how in the world I am going to write that down in the Dispensary book: ah mother, there is a funny side to it sometimes.

I shall never forget one day; the MO asked what kind of dressing one of the patients had on his leg; for the life of me, I could not just remember then whether it was Hydrog[1] Ammon Oil ointment or Red Lotion.[2] I said at first it was one thing, then another; but at last I remembered rightly, and told him. I had not had time to dress him before the doctor came through; and there are so many with different dressings, that I assure you, you must not be asleep on the wards; there are thousands of things to remember.

I only have 21 patients now. All the beds are numbered from 1 to 26

No 1 has internal trouble, and was partly operated on

---

1. Possibly hydrogen.
2. A zinc-based ointment used to treat leg ulcers.

yesterday morning: last night the MO told me to give him a light breakfast this morning, as he would be for the theatre again: so about 11 am to-day, he was operated on again: but he told me when I was writing the evening report that he felt all right.

No 2, has a sprained ankle; so that meant quite a bit of work for me this morning. I had to pad a splint reaching from his toes to his thigh, then cover all with wool and bandage firmly; that job cannot be done in a minute: as the foot and leg must be in correct position on that splint; with padding under knee, then I had to put foot between two sand bags, so that it wouldn't tip over in bed, then an iron cage had to be placed over feet and legs to prevent bed clothes from disarranging the splint.

No 3 was appendicitis; he had to be dressed for theatre operation; which meant the getting ready, such as long theatre stockings coming half way [up] the thigh, a pneumonia jacket over chest and back tied under arms with four strings, and on the shoulder with three strings; then I put two open back shirts on him besides: after he was operated on, they transferred him to D2 ward: we do not keep appendicitis in G3.

No 4 has had a bad finger for 4 weeks: last week he had the nail removed; but still it is no better. I just put a clean piece of gauze on it, and wool, bandaged it, then he had to go to be Xrayd; after he came back, I had to put a Boric Oint[ment] Foment[3] on it, then Jacouet; then wool

---

3. An antiseptic of moderate power which is applied in powder or strong solutions to wounds, ulcers, abscesses – an excellent choice to use on the bad finger Fanny treated.

and bandage; these wounds are small, yet mother you can judge the amount of time they take.

No 5 has a foment on (R) leg and (L) thigh, ointment on four places on the legs then wool and bandage.

No 6 is another appendicitis, which came in to-day. I am sure in the morning I shall have to get him ready for the theatre: he must not eat anything: but drink.

No 7 patient went yesterday to Duty; cured of Synovictis Knee.

No 8 has a very bad finger for weeks: he had the top opened. At first we gave him finger baths every morning; then fomented it; then the MO changed it to dry dressing; then from that he changed it to foments again; now he has it done with ointment; but this morning the MO said he would probe it to morrow morning; poor patient, he got weak the last time it was probed, and had to have his face washed; so I have that to prepare for in the morning.

No 9: has Injury to Ribs: he really is on no treatment, except rest.

(No 10) has the most extraordinary feet I ever saw. He says they have been like it more or less since he was 8 years of age: how in the world he has walked and marched since the war, I cannot see: the bottoms of his feet, heels especially were all covered over like a canker potato, exactly the same: black in colour. Sister said that never in all her life had she ever seen anything like it except a seedy rock. Well! his feet had to be soaked in hot soapy water twice a day, 2 hrs each time then dried, and pieces taken off with forceps. I used to spread a rubber sheet on the bed, and then start to work; finally he could do it himself, thank goodness: to-day, he soaked them one hour, then I rubbed then thoroughly with vaseline, and bandaged them.

No 11 is Hemorhoids [*sic*].

No 12 is empty, thank goodness: but to morrow isn't come yet.

No 13   "   "   "   ".

No 14   "   "   "   ".

No 15 is a bad toe, which has to be cleaned with Ensol, then a layer of ointment, then gauze with Indiform[4] probed around the nail: some of these boys do not murmur: I am sure I should scream the tent down.

No 16 has been a very bad elbow: but it is improving rapidly now. The arm is yet a bit bent; although he lifts heavy weights. The MO ordered him to carry full buckets; he is now quite able to go around and make beds with me; but mother it was a nasty elbow at the beginning: and before he came to hospital, he tried to remedy it himself with bread poultices; however he scalded the elbow; poor thing, I suppose he must have put the poultice on boiling. He is now on dry gauze, wool and bandage.

No 17 is empty.

No 18 has had his toes operated on: he has them tied to an iron cage, with a steel splint bandaged on the side of his foot; the twelfth day, the stitches will be taken out of the toes; he has now been six days: we do not touch him

---

4. A white powder produced by the reaction between formaldehyde and acetylsalicylic acid, soluble in cold water; it was used as an anti-neuralgic (painkiller) and an anti-rheumatic.

except make his bed and rub his back with methylated spirit and powder so that he won't get bed sore: of course his feet has [sic] to be re-tied to the cage: he had the left foot done first, the right one has yet to be done.

No 19 is going to Convalescent camp to morrow: he had a boil opened in his back: an awful, awful boil: they made an opening + shaped in the back about 1 inch and a half each way: he had to have Ensol dressing every morning and the body bandaged.

No 20 is a South-African Staff Sergeant: his is a discoloured ankle: I put a large piece of ointment on it, then bandaged it tightly with a crepe bandage.

No 21 had a boil opened on the back, and another further down the spine. He was only brought from the theatre a little while when the blood came through the bandage: I told Sister about it, and that I had repacked him. I went down to dinner. Sister went up to see him: he had bled most horribly; she again repacked him: I came on after dinner, tidied the beds, and his too of course, then went down to Sisters ward to do a heavy patient. One of G3 boys came down for me saying he was bleeding: I ran up, My word! I never saw anything like it. I went for Sister in D2, as my own Sister was gone to her dinner. It was blood everywhere. She wrote a note to Capt Milne, who immediately came up, took off all dressings, and with the forceps took out a clot of blood the size of a fish's heart, the largest heart I had ever seen: blood spouted over the locker and every thing. Oh! it was horrible. The rubber sheet was covered, his white sheet had to be changed, his shirt also: I assure you mother, no flies were on me, when I had to get things ready for the doctor: but the boy is improving; and was up yesterday for half an hour; but when I took his temperature, I had to send him to bed again; to-day he was up a bit longer.

I foment his shoulder and thigh, Ensol dressing on his back in two places. He is also drinking stout - a bottle every day.

No 22 — had an abscess in his shoulder opened, which is done with Ensol.

No 23 — had the top of his finger taken off with a circular saw: but had again to be operated on: he has a picric dressing on that.

No 24 — has varicose veins bandaged with crepe elastic bandages:

Mother you should have these crepe bandages for your knees: they are splendid.

No 25 — is a shell-shock boy: of course after 3 days his speech came back; but still he is excitable: we now have him for patient orderly: he is a good boy: does anything at all I ask him.

No 26 is frost-bitten feet and hands: I get tired of cutting off dead skin; he is on ointment, and has one very bad sore on his foot: he also has a cough.

That will give you an idea of the work in G3. Of course complaints differ. To-day we had 21 patients, to-morrow we may be filled. These patients have been up the line previously; but now are no longer fit for front line; so they get work at the base.

These dressings have to be done before I go to my dinner, in addition to the general tidying up of the ward, the Diet sheet to fill in, the Diet Book to write,

Dispensaries to send for, the Treatment Book with No of Beds, Patients, Temperatures, Diagnosis, Treatment to fill in; the dressing bowls and instruments to be sterilized.

I wish you could take a peep in the ward. G3 has no white counter panes: but just the dark brown blankets. Matron says she may give me counterpanes. The canvas is old and dirty. Sometimes the stoves smoke abominably.

The other day when I was down to dinner, Matron came through the wards examining the ceiling. I know there was lots of smoke on my roof; since it had not been swept down since Xmas Eve: really there is no time to bother with sweeping down tent roofs. However she got the up patients to sweep the soot off, regardless of the beds: you can fancy mother the state of the blankets: I had to brush every bed in the first half of the tent.

G3 is divided in the centre; but I am doing my best to get it taken down: it will improve the ward wonderfully. I have spoken to the Sergeant of the ward about it; also the Sergt Major, who has interviewed the Colonel, who will shortly see about it. There is so much red tape to go through when one wants to get anything done.

Matron told me yesterday that I would soon be going in the mess: she also suggested that I would go as Home Sister in the Mess, that is, superintending meals etc. She asked me if I had done anything like it before. I said "No", except at home. Then she said she would give the position to a striped Sister. The idea of giving me that to do. I didn't want it at all: but I really thought I was going to help the Mess V.A.D's waiting on the tables etc.

Matron told my "Sister" about it: but Sister insisted on my keeping G3 ward; which was exceedingly good of her. I expect after I get back from my leave, that I shall either go on Night Duty again, or work in the Mess. My duty on nights is drawing along.

I have not said anything about poor Vince. I got a letter from his mother and Ray: and will answer both shortly. Tell Aunt Sarah I shall do my best for her. Did she get my letter. I used to think that perhaps Vince and I would spend our vacation together. I think of him when I see the drafts go up the line, headed by the Officers. I knew when he was sick that he must be more than slightly wounded, as he never once wrote me, otherwise I should have had a very long letter. It was the Battle of Cambrai[5] he was wounded in. All our boys got knocked out. Gas was used a lot. Poor Vince's wound was gassed as well. I cannot, for a minute realize that he is dead.

Good night mother.

From your loving daughter Fannie.

---

5. Actually he died of wounds inflicted during fighting at the village of Masnières on the way to take the final objective, the town of Cambrai. After the Battle of Cambrai had ended the Regiment received word that "His Majesty the King had been pleased to approve the grant of the title 'Royal' to the Newfoundland Regiment." No other regiment of the British Army was to receive such a distinction during World War I while fighting was in progress. On just two previous occasions was the prefix "Royal" conferred on a British army regiment during wartime.

Dear Lil,

It is now ten minutes past seven, Sunday evening. I am on duty, but not very busy. I am moved from G3 where we were exceedingly busy, scarcely had a moment to call your own: but owing to shortness of staff, I am being moved to what is called the "Extension".

"Extension" consists of I1 Ward, L1, L2 and Dressing Tent.

I never had such an easy time since I started nursing.

Sister Horrocks is in charge of all these tents, and I am her only V.A.D. She very seldom comes through L1, L2 and Dressing Tent; but her resting place is in I1: that is a hut of 52 beds.

G3 was Local Surgical; but these others are Convoy Surgical, except I1 that is Convoy Medical.

To-day, we have moved all patients from L2 into L1, as I hear that a front line tent is going to be taken down and the patients transferred to L2. Our Canadian patient orderly is sleeping alone in L2 to-night: somebody must sleep in an open ward: I hope he doesn't freeze in there.

I wish you could see me scribbling this in L1, leaning over a white board table: the up patients crowded around the stove to keep themselves warm; we haven't every comfort in the Extension I assure you.

I must stop now as I have hot water bottles to fill in L1 and some Aspirin Tablets and Phenasetin[1] Tablets to give to P.U.O. patients. P.U.O. stands for "patients under observation". We have many of them in the medical wards. It is a sort of Trench fever and Rheumatism: they complain of pains in the shin bones, lower part of back and head.

To night I brought some chocolates to the poor things; chocolates that came in one of the boxes that was sent to Vince.

—

Wednesday night

You see I did not finish the letter on Sunday night. It is now nine o'clock. Nurse Taylor and I just came from Con. Camp (convalescent camp). A man lectured there, or rather recited some poetry on "A Sergeant and a Private". It started from the time the private enlisted. It seems that this private had a very rough time under the Sergeant. When the time came to go over the top, the Sergeant had both eyes blown out, and the private being near crawled to him; the Sergeant wished to take his hand before he died. However, the private was fatally wounded: both chatted together for a while on the next world where there was no war. Well Lil it was a most thrilling recitation: the blood went cold all through my body. In addition to that the

---

1. An analgesic (pain reliever).

band struck up, playing very thundering pieces and the American Anthem; then the whole audience stood until it was finished. The band also played a part of the "Swanee River", and "Tramp, Tramp, Tramp the boys are marching", and "Nearer my God to Thee". It was thrilling. I can't write any more. My pen is gone dry.

Good night from Fan.

10 Gen Hos
Rouen
9/18[1]

Dear Mother

Just a line to say I am taking my leave tomorrow morning. I leave Rouen about 8:30 am, must be at Rue De Vern Station 9:15 am. I am going to Cannes, South of France. It is two days run by train. I spend one night in Paris. Another Canadian from No 8 Hospital is going.

I wish you could see one packing. It is now 11 pm. I have a candle lit on table; but have to blow it out, if I think Matron or Super Night Sister is prowling about; then relight it again.

My room is in a perfect muddle. The last thing I couldn't find was (I've just had to blow out the candle again thank heavens, the night Sister has made her last round) my red-cross arm brassard. I hunted every crook and corner finally found it between some books. My orders came through D.D.M.S. office night before last. I must leave Cannes again on the 25th.

I just made myself a cup of chocolate, some of my Xmas eatables.

This is the first leave I've had since started nursing.

---

1. This letter was written from Rouen, just prior to her departure for Cannes early March 1918. The intended date for this letter is March 9, 1918.

We are supposed to get leave every 6 months. I've got to do a bit of hustling in the morning.

Ask Lil and Bish if they don't wish they were coming too.

I wrote Joseph a long time ago. I had a letter from Aunt Aggie and shall answer it while down South.

I shall visit Monte Carlo: We go through Marseilles; but we can only go a few steps on Italy borderline; as there are sentries every where.

Good night mother. Love to all.

Will write when arrive South.

Your loving daughter Fanny.

Received your letter yesterday. Would like also to hear from Bish and Susie.

Cannes
22/3/18

Friday

Dear Mother,

I am still at beautiful Cannes.[1] It has been terribly hot to-day; I think I shall take a salt water bath on Monday, providing the weather is as good as it has been recently.

Today Sister Valentine and I started at 10 a.m. to go to St. Paul, a village on the top of a mountain. Of course we knew we had to go to Antibes at first, and from there to Cagnes;[2] then walk 7 kilometres. Well! we got to Antibes all right: then enquired about tram for Cagnes: I said to a woman on the sidewalk "Quel heur tram, pour Nice" (What time was the tram for Nice?) She said "demi-une" (half past one). It was then only about a quarter to twelve: we decided to go down to the edge of the Mediterranean and wait. It was really lunch time, but we proposed to have lunch at Cagnes. After sitting a while on a very hard seat in the broiling sun, I suggested to Sister that I should go up town & get some fruit. I went up street; and down street: but my word! they were so frightfully expensive: I just had ½ dozen apples for myself and an orange for Sister which I

---

1. A town on France's Mediterranean coast known as a luxurious holiday spot. Apparently a hotel there was allocated to military and paramilitary personnel on leave.
2. A small town along the same coast as Cannes situated between Antibes and Nice.

paid 4 pence[3] for: just think! 4 pence for one orange. These French peoples will be millionaires, made precisely off Sisters. They exceed the limit in prices altogether.

However: we munched away until tram came in view; we laughingly took it; but found to our dismay when paying the fare that the tram we took went only to the terminus and not to Nice at all. Oh dear! oh dear! it was getting late and we did so want to get to St. Paul. We could not get off and take another back as there was only the one tram going back and forth; nothing would do, but that we should go on to the terminus. There we got off and found we had to wait 3/4 of an hour for it to start again: by this time we were getting well worked up I assure you mother. To pass away the time, I went into a gorgeous garden facing a wonderfully large hotel, walked about viewing the beautiful flowers until nearly starting time. Eventually we started, and arrived at Cagnes about ten minutes to four, allowing us no time to walk to St. Paul. We had lunch at a restaurant there; as a matter-of-fact, you could not give it the name of lunch. I asked for "froide viande" (cold meat). She said she could not give me any then. Sister asked [for] bread and butter; but she wasn't allowed to sell any until 6 o'clock; neither could we have milk with our tea; but thank goodness we got sugar to put into it, that is a rare treat; but of course we always get it at L'Esterel Hotel where we stay.

We left Cagnes 10 minutes to five; but had to wait ever so long at Antibes for a Cannes tram. We knew we had to be in by 7 p.m dinner. When we got into Cannes town something happened to our tram, which hindered

---

3. Four pence in 1918 is the equivalent of $1.12 in 2006 Canadian dollars.

us umpteen minutes; eventually we had to take another tram, arriving at L'Esterel Hotel at 7 pm sharp. I rushed up stairs, tore off my street uniform, and jumped into my grey alpaca uniform and cap; hooking cuffs on way down stairs, as bell had gone, and perhaps Lady Giffard would be waiting to say "grace". I want to be punctual while I'm here, although at Rouen I am always told about being late.

My travelling papers showed that I was to leave Cannes on 25th: but a Sister who was asked to stay until 26th informed Lady Giffard she preferred going on 25th for special reasons; adding that as I had been sick I undoubtedly would take her place; so you see mother I shall be here a day longer than I thought I would. Happy thought. I don't care whether Rouen matron is agreeable to it; I am going to risk it.

I wish mother you could see the exterior and interior of this Hotel: can a palace be better?

The drawing room is "comfort" in every sense of the word. I sleep in same room with Miss Oliver a Canadian V.A.D. The floor of our bedroom is red brick tiled and polished with a mat by my bed-side and hers and by the commode. The commode, mantel piece, bureau, bed-table are all marble topped; by my bed side on a little table stands an electric lamp with red globe which when I turn off centre lights, I turn this one on to read. There is also a wardrobe with mirror the whole length of it: over the mantel piece is another awfully large mirror: the window opens with a very beautiful scenery: the Mediterranean. Every thing in the hotel is white; all the walls and ceiling in dining room and sitting room. There are no dark doors at all. Every thing is just grand as could be: the halls are red carpeted.

I don't know where I shall go to morrow: I should like to go to Nice again. I think I shall go by train this time.

A New Zealand Sister was sitting opposite me at this table to night writing: she said to me "I envy you girls being able to go home on leave". I (my pen is gone dry) said to her "I couldn't get home, that was why I was down here": she said, "Didn't you come from England" I said "No, from NFLD"; of course then we chatted over things. She had had several NFLD boys in her wards; they were typical colonials; the colonials seem much freer than the English Tommies.

There is a V.A.D here from SJAB[4] at Etaples; I enquired about poor Vincent; but she was not in the officers' ward; but will find particulars about him when she goes back and let me know. I have been enquiring if there were any from 48 C.C.S. here, but as yet I have met no one.

I must go to bed; I am nearly the last left in sitting room; I was just asked if I wished to have breakfast in bed; being so rare a treat I said "Yes".

Miss Oliver is getting up at 5:30 am to go to Menton.[5] These Canadians got no end of money; they are paid extraordinarily well. Next Friday, I shall be in hospital again. I heard an inkling I was going on Medical Lines again: I hope American Sister asks Matron for me to come to Extension Tents with her on Surgical Side.

Good night mother.

Your daughter Fanny.

---

3. St. John Ambulance Brigade.
4. The French city on the Côte d'Azur nearest to the Italian border.

Easter Sunday Morning.

Dear Mother:

I am going to Church at 11:15 am, for I am so terribly tired. We are awfully busy, nearly killed since this last rush: If this war does not soon end there won't be a man living on the face of the earth. It is brutal; it is cold-blooded murder; it is hell upon earth. Ah! If you could only see and go through what we do mother; it is enough to drive one mad.

I am on duty in the Compound. I shall never forget these days. Convoys are coming in all night long; patients are vacating in the midst of it. I have four wards with a little help once in a while; if this rush continues, some of us will give out altogether.

I came back from "leave" five nights ago; arriving at Rouen 8 p.m. Matron sent me on night duty at 10 p.m. same night: oh! my head was so heavy from travelling; had been on train two days, the second night on train I did not sleep at all, it was so cold.

From the time I went on duty at 10 p.m., I did not stop a minute until 8 am next morning, except to have a cup of tea at 12 pm.

I say again this war is simply horrible. What a blessing some of these boys mothers do not see their husbands and sons.

Sometimes an orderly comes through to help me a little bit. I have to wait on the patients such as giving them drinks, the bed pans, then perhaps the stretcher bearer comes in for a man to go to the theatre to have his wounds opened, or his hand off, whatever the case may be. Well! if he is a helpless patient, I've got to try to do the best I can to get him on the stretcher or run for an orderly, or look for Sister to help; then when he is taken away, his bed has to be made into an operation bed ready for him again: just as you finish that in comes the stretcher bearers for another one; by the time he is ready to go, the other one is brought back, then put on his bed, a vomiting basin given him, and watched at intervals for vomiting, hemorrhages etc.; then probably we are warned by the Sergt that a convoy is going out at such a time to England. He names the patients in each ward who are going; I have these to prepare for travelling: I tell you mother its nothing easy to dress a helpless patient, putting vests, shirts, cardigan, jacket, drawers, pants; sometimes you can only get one leg in the drawers, and only one sleeve of the jacket; then one must see that everything as regards their papers go with them. These papers indicate when they are taken sick, to what hospital they are sent, his name, regiment, rank, where wounded etc; essential papers.

Well, while getting them ready for the stretcher bearers to take them to the reception tent before getting on the travelling boat, perhaps a convoy has just come down from the line; in they come, stretcher after stretcher; oh my! their clothes have to be cut off; shirts pants and everything, such a state of blood and mud; they are then bathed; and one has to handle them very very carefully especially if he [is] shot in the head. No head case is allowed to sit up at all. Some of them can't see at all; all smashed to pieces; one poor poor boy lying day after day with eyes bandaged. Think of them blind for life and so young.

I have been so tired towards morning that I could scarcely walk; the bottoms of my feet are like boils; my first ward on night duty this year was C1. Just as we had one man washed and shrouded ready to be taken to the mortuary, I was sent to go to another ward to help sister prepare another for the mortuary. Next evening I was told to watch a man until his last breath went. I never thought mother that I would do what I have done. I went behind the screens and stayed with him until he died. Oh the pitiful sights, the worn faces: one man asked just before he died when he would see his mother.

Next night in the midst of our rush I was sent to special a man. He was wounded in buttock, left arm, abdomen. His arm was in "Thomas" splint; that is bound on steel rods:[1] the poor thing was raving at times. We were giving him a saline injection, but gave it up: he died about 7 pm.

When I came off duty this morning, one of our patients was slowly fading. You cannot realize mother what we go through.

I have been to Church; both going and coming I saw them taking stretchers with the 'Union Jack' on them; you know what that means.

It is now 1 am: I must go to bed as we get up are rather called at 6:30 pm.

---

1. A rigid splint constructed of steel bars that are curved to fit the involved limb and held in place by a cast or rigid bandage.

One of the patients was telling me about this last push when the Germans drove them back; he said you could see them coming; as fast as you knock one down another took his place, there was no end to them, at last they had to retire; the Germans are getting the best of it. Out of one of the boy's battalion only 9 came back; they tell us it is murder. Of course we get it right from the persons who are engaged in the battle and not from the papers. Another said he just went with his company to dig a trench; they were not fighting men; but found when they had finished, they had to hold the line; and he said he was no good at all, not able to do anything of the kind. One old man, got knocked about a bit; he couldn't run he said like the younger ones: poor old chap he must have lain in the cold quite a while; he is so wheezy. The Germans nearly encircled them.

To hear the draughts go up the line every evening singing and cheering, band playing. Sister said yesterday it made her blood run cold; they go up never to return, except to come maimed for life. I don't think I have written like this before mother, which plainly says things are much worse.

Paris was shelled from the Germans 75 mile gun. As we came through one street there, the chauffeur showed us where bombs had dropped

Sister Coneys came through Paris yesterday; one shell dropped 20 yards from their ambulance, she was down South when I was there; but I left a few days before. I went into two churches while in Paris; perhaps it might have been one of these that was shelled.

The Casualty Clearing Stations are bombed; we have

nearly twenty sisters, who had to leave for their life, saved nothing only what they wore; shells flying every where. They say at one place there are 6000 wounded tommies. waiting to be sent somewhere, walking about in horrid conditions: of course if these C.C.S. had not been bombed we would not have been so busy; this now is like a Casualty Clearing Station. Boys are dying for want of attention; they cannot be attended to before being sent down here; wounds lying so long of course must kill them. It is horrible mother.

Good bye. Nothing would induce me to give it up mother.

Fannie.

I am sending Lil a collar.[2]

These are the hymns we had this morning.

No 167	An Australian
No 165	minister. Very
No 499	splendid sermon.
No 134	

Did you get the boots I sent. The pullies were for you: the high boots for Lil, the others for you. Did I send a piece of shrapnel.

---

2. This postscript was written on the back of the letter.

Carte Postale

Nov. 2-18
Borders of Italy

Dear Mother,

Oh it is gorgeous here; I am standing on this bridge. We could not get into Italy. The Chinese guard allowed us to go to the end of the bridge this time. I wish you could see the Americans, British, Australians, Canadians standing on this bridge

6. - GRIMALDI (Italia) - Servizio alla Frontiera - Ponte san Luigi
Carabinieri et Doganieri Italiani e Francesi

Carte Postale

Sunday, Apr.27/19

Dear Mother,

I had this postal card in Paris. Isn't it a very pathetic one?

You see I am still in Rouen, expecting orders any moment to go. Five sisters went this morning at 5 am. There are only about 40 of us left out of a staff of over 100.

Excuse lead pencil mother. Sister Gibbs borrowed my ink & she is now in bed, so I can't very well go to her room, although she sleeps next to me.

I am nursing Germans. Two died and one has been delirious all day. He is on ½ oz brandy every 4 hours, and oxygen 10 minutes. He is so young. Good night mother.

Love from Fanny.

MUSÉE DE L'ARMÉE — Église des Invalides — « NOS MARTYRS pour le Droit et la Liberté »
Par Joseph Aubert (1916)
ARMY MUSEUM — Invalid Church — « OUR MARTYRS for Right and Freedom », by Joseph Aubert (1916)

74 Eccleston Sq.
V.A.D. Hostel.
July 27-19
London

Sunday Evening

Dear Mother,

Here I am still waiting to go to Constantinople. I don't know what time the crowd for going will be gathered together. I hear four of the number were not medically fit to go East owing to dysentery etc, there.

I have been to Church twice to day for a wonder. I have not been much of a Church [goer] since I became a V.A.D.: we have had so few chances of going: I seem to have got out of Church going, like Lil was when she came from Sydney.

This morning Nurse MacLean & I went to St.Paul's. I sat middle way up the aisle, and scarcely heard half a dozen words the minister said: but I did watch the styles. People were coming in and going out all the time the service was going on; I assure you mother, it is not at all like our Church at home. I could have got up from my seat and gone to any part of the Cathedral if I wished: I did get up after a while and wen[t] eight or nine seats up: oh! it is funny: the people are never settled in there. I prefer our own Church for services: the building is indeed very wonderful.

This evening we went to Eccleston Church, just across from this Hostel. I liked it there very much: the sermon was certainly good, taken from Kings (I think) 11th chapter, 17-19 verses.

We have just finished supper of lettuce salad and bully & coffee & two small pieces of bread.

Oh! how I long for some pork and beans, pork and cabbage and pork soup: and pea soup, beef and potatoes etc. I miss them yet. We have the same thing nearly every day here. Thank goodness, when I can get somewhere that we are not rationed.

Nearly every night MacLean and I go down to Lyons or Victoria Street to get a cup of something. I always have cocoa and she has tea.

I cannot tell you my Constantinople address this time: but will on next letter. Did you get the $10 I sent you and the $5 I sent to Lil?

I sent Lil an old gray jersey in June, also Joseph and Wilfred a scrap book.

A short while ago I sent you a black crepe-dichane blouse, and Lil some silk for one.

The other day I sent Lil a little black straw hat which is worn turned up at the back and out the front, and a brown leather pocket book: this week I am sending her a beautiful dressing gown for resting Sunday afternoons in her bedroom; it is a pretty thing. I hope she gets it all right. Mother the snaps I send you with my name on the back of them, will you keep them for me?, as they were given to me by some friends.

Snap marked (4) are different nationalities. First boy standing is a Canadian, (2) a South African, his badge being a deer's head in a circle. (3) Newfoundland. (4) New Zealand. (5) Australian. (6) Scotch.

We are out on the deck of "Prince George" going up Lock Lomond. It was a very dull day, raining at times: I thought the picture would be no good at all: but I see the forms are there. The last boy sitting owned the camera: he sent me all the snaps you see that size. Was it not good of him? I shall send him some of what I am printing.

I am also enclosing a leaflet, given to me on Victory March Day.

Oh, Mother! I wish you could have seen the parade.

MacLean and I were going to leave the Hostel at 9 am: when I heard some one else was coming with us: of course she had to get ready. I knew her of old, having waited ever so long for her to go to a theatre one night, and had after all to go on and leave her: when we were coming down stairs, met some one else who said she would like to come with us. Great Scott! I thought we would never get out. I was on pins and needles all the time, knowing that every inch of ground would be taken up down at Grosvenor Gardens where we were going.

However, we got off at last to find the police would-n't allow us through the crowd: we had to go around the Square and come to the Gardens another way.

Some lady another was standing at the gate and would say "where are you from?" Our pass word would be 74 Eccleston Sq. We were let inside. To get a better view I stood up on the iron palings, stuck my feet between the spikes and rested my back against a tree. We waited there from 9 o'clock until 12 o'clock. You can imagine my poor feet and back: they ached I assure you.

The procession was splendid. The Americans led: then Belgians next: then Canadians (I think the regiments went in Alphabetical order).

The French looked very splendid, with their flags swinging from their bugles. Very thrilling. General Foch[1] headed his crew of course. Then were hundreds of naval boys headed by David Beatty.[2] Sir Douglas Haig[3] appeared to be a bit shy.

I must send you a paper of it all.

Nursing Sisters and a few VADs, Waacs,[4] Wrens,[5] etc paraded. The parade they marched was six miles:

Oh Mother! the cheering. You can not realize what it was like; the splendour of their dresses, flags innumerable.

London was decorated beyond description. A monument was erected at Whitehall in memory of the fallen. Pall Mall was elaborately done.

Buckingham Palace aglow with flags.

---

1. Ferdinand Foch (1851–1929), French general, was named Allied Supreme Commander in March 1918, a position he held to the end of the War.
2. Sir David Beatty (1871–1936), British admiral, became Commander of the Grand Fleet of the Royal Navy in November 1916. He received the surrender of the German High Fleet off the coast of Scotland on November 21, 1918.
3. Sir Douglas Haig (1861–1928), British general, was appointed Commander-in-Chief of the British Expeditionary Force on December 10, 1915. He commanded the British forces, including the Newfoundland Regiment, at the Battle of the Somme.
4. Women's Army Auxiliary Corps, a voluntary service of the British Army. They worked behind the lines as clerks, telephonists, waitresses, cooks, gardeners, and telegraphists.
5. The Women's Royal Naval Service (WRNS) recruited women for the same reason and similar tasks as the WAACs.

Good night mother: will tell you more about it; but it would take hours to describe it.

Your loving daughter Fannie.

Have not heard from home for months. (Silly asses at Marseilles sent my letters to Newfoundland).

52 Gen. Hos.
Mashlak[1]
Army Black Sea
Constantinople
Nov.18/19

Dear Mother:-

This is our first day of winter: it has been dreadfully cold, snowing, blowing and raining.

It is now getting dark. I only wish you could take a peep in this marquee. My candle is nearly burnt out; I know it won't last five minutes longer: I had to borrow half a candle last night. Oh! this is our issue candle night; every Tuesday we are issued with two candles, and they are supposed to last a whole week; but mine don't. Miss Moore is sitting in my corner sewing: to keep ourselves warm we have a little oil stove burning: I shall heat some water when I come back from dinner to fill a hot water bottle. I notice Moore's candle is nearly gone; then we shall sit in darkness or by the stove light until 8 o'clock. You see the days are short, it's no wonder our candles go;

---

1. The name of a hunting lodge that belonged to the Sultanate. It was located outside the urban area of Constantinople toward the northeast, in parkland on the European side of the Bosphorus. With additions from many Sultans, Mashlak included four mansions as well as other pavilions and structures by the end of the nineteenth century. The lay-out and peaceful surroundings were an excellent choice for a military hospital.

but just imagine only two candles for a whole week; why! it's perfectly ridiculous. Moore is trying to sew; but she will soon have to put it down for want of light.

Last night, we made coffee and tea on this little stove, boiling about a pint of water at a time until we got enough for five cups. Mrs. Morton, Mallet & Moore sat in my room; some one said my room was the Kitchen. Well! after our coffee; we started to play cards: then Miss Thompson came in to see if Moore was going up to the mess room to the M.O.'s (Medical Officers) dance. I asked Thompson if she would have a cup of coffee, hoping she would say No; hang it all! she said she would like a cup. I had to put my ½ pint saucepan on again. However we played 6 or 7 games of whist.

I do hope I won't be as cold in bed to night as last night; although I slept in my heavy dressing gown and bed stockings. The wind blows in through the end and side. Night before last; I had to get up and move my things from the side of the tent; Moore had to move her bed; the end of tent came unfastened; it was simply terrible. I never in all my life heard anything like it: the flapping of the canvas is enough to craze one. Poor Moore she has never roughed it before; but Morton & I have gone through similar ordeals in France; only there; were things one went through that nothing in the world will blot it out. Ah! those days of war.

I received your letter 4 days ago. Glad to hear you got money all right: but mother, when I send you money for yourself I want you to have it. It makes me vexed to know you don't spend it on things for yourself. Did you get the $1 note I sent in a letter a while ago.

I hope it isn't raining and snowing to morrow: one never knows, it may be a beautifully warm day.

Good night. Thank goodness, dinner is earlier to night.

Your loving daughter Fannie.

Take care of yourself mother.

82 Gen. Hos.
Army Black Sea.
G.S.V.A.D. Hd. Qrs
Constantinople
4-12-19
[December 4, 1919]

Dear Mother:-

Xmas is drawing along: I am not sending any pres-
ents, it is so very far; and there is every possible chance of
their getting lost. Day before yesterday I bought a postal
card of the Shah's palace in the city for you: but I cannot
find it anywhere; I seem never to be able to find my
things: they seem to be scattered everywhere: although
my room is just a few feet long.

We are now in the city, in an extensive building. I
have not been up to Mashlak since we came here. I am
working in the clothing stores with Mrs. Flood: she is an
old time soldier as it were. The corporal who was in
charge of the stores was demobbed a couple of days after
we came here, leaving everything in Mrs. Flood's charge,
and that includes a great great deal. I am learning from
her, so that when she is off duty I can take full charge. The
work is like this. In our store we have:

Khaki suits.
gray socks.

towels.
woolen shirts
cotton & wollen drawers,
braces. Men's eastern hats.
puttees. boots men's sizes
singlets, cardigan jackets.
Khahi caps.
Khaki overcoats.
razors, knives, forks, spoons,
combs, tooth brushes
chevrons for Lance corporals,
Corporals & Sergeants.
brass buttons, bone buttons,
Red Crosses;

that is nearly the extent of the "Clothing store".

The "Pack Store" is joined to it only we don't have to go in there.

If an R.A.M.C boy or a patient comes in to exchange a pair of boots. First of all we have to look and see if the boots are serviceable; if not, we don't change them: if they are bad we throw them into an unserviceable pile and give him another pair: he then signs his name to a paper or form printed for those purposes. First of all we write his number, name rank in black ink; things we exchange are put down in red ink; then he lastly puts his name to it; this is done with every article that is exchanged: if a patient is going back to his own unit we tell him they will fit him out there: but if he is going to the Rest Camp we fit him out in our store. We do not change combs for patients but only for the Personnel, that is the R.A.M.C. staff.

When they come with razors to be exchanged, these also have to be seen if they are unserviceable; you can imagine now what the work is like. Sometimes the boys come in, and they have not yet had their winter issue; that means we have to take in their summer khaki drill and give them khaki cloth suit, woolen underwear. I wish you could see some of their things they bring in to exchange; holes in the heels of the socks etc: it is laughable some times. Everything that goes out of the store is taken down, the same with things that come in; there is a lot of book keeping done here; the other night after Corporal left, Mrs. Flood and I were down at the books until 11 o'clock at night; all papers are sent to the Quarter Master's office for his examination, and if he approves of it he signs them, then they are brought back to us again, then we know we can carry on: it is a great responsibility: but I like it. All the unserviceable things are corrected, baled, ticketed, sent back to Ordnance in the city: we work the books in turn & cheque [sic] each other: the other night, we found a patient had been issued with a cap comforter; it was in the ledger as an issue and not as a receipt; we spent ever so long over that one thing, wondering where that cap comforter came from, if there was none in stock: so next day Mrs. Flood told the Quarter Master about it; he said there must have been one knocking about and the Corporal issued it to the patient: why in the world he put it in the ledger I don't know: it gave us some worrying moments.

An order was sent in the other day saying a Russian patient was coming down and we had to give him a partially worn "Stand Up Kit": that means everything one wears at one time. The poor Russian had been a Turkish

Prisoner of War for a year: and it is only since he came into our hospital that the British found out that he was a prisoner of war: so he is now released and going to Petrograd; but mother he has been terribly wounded in back and hips and appears quite a cripple now. His people were Bolsheviks: in their terrible struggles his parents, brother and sister were killed: he looked so pitiful.

The Armenian boy who helps in book-keeping in Pack Stores was telling me his father was massacred by the Turks during the War.

I cannot write any more: two of the girls are talking to me & jerking me to listen to them.

So Good Night Mother. It's impossible to write.

Your loving daughter
Fannie.

63 St. George Sq.

Victoria.

Central V.A.D Hostel

Sunday, 21st[1]

Dear Mother:-

Arrived in London Thursday evening about 3:30 p.m. from Southampton. Left Constantinople on the 4th November. Had a lovely trip through the Mediterranean: became a bit loppy as we came through Bay of Biscay. The Channel was splendid: we came from Southampton to London by rail: Friday a.m. at 10 o'clock, Miss Henderson and I reported at Hd. Qrs in Berkeley Street. I interviewed one of the clerks who did not know anything about my repatriation; but told me I had better wait to see Lady Oliver,[2] who was expected in at 11 a.m: fortunately Lady Oliver came early: she gave me a letter to take to High Commissioners of Newfoundland[3] in Victoria Street: Oh dear that meant another long tram ride. However we did it. The man there knew all about my repatriation. What do

---

1. The month and the year were not written on the letter, but it is evident from the postmark on the envelope that the date was November 21, 1920.
2. Lady Oliver was a member of the Joint VAD Commitment appointed to oversee the work of the VAD, the Territorial Forces Association, the British Red Cross Society, and the Order of St. John of Jerusalem during the War.
3. Sir Edgar Rennie Bowring (1858–1943) was Newfoundland's first High Commissioner to London, a post held from 1918 to 1922.

you think mother; there is a boat sailing on the 30th or thereabouts of this month. Good luck wasn't it? I finished with him, then had to go again to Berkeley Street to tell Lady Oliver the result of the interview.

I then expressed a desire to go to Etaples to visit poor Vincent's grave before coming home. Lady Oliver advised me to go to [War] Graves Commission on Baker Street. We got there: I was disappointed to hear that I should have to pay all expenses myself: After looking through a book to get an estimate of expenses, he said for 4 days including everything would cost me £5. I gave the idea up of course: but I really think I could do the trip in less than 4 days: however I shall go to the Y.M. people myself to morrow and find out particulars; but I mustn't risk missing my passage to N.F.L.D.

I shall wire you when I arrive in St. John's.

We had rather a nice time in the Rio Pardo coming: Were at Malta for a few hours: went on shore: I rather like Malta: it is so particularly clean.

We anchored off Gibraltar: I never imagined the Rock of Gibraltar is like it is.

This is Sunday: I don't feel at all like going out: but I suppose I should go to Westminster Abbey or St. Paul's. I don't think I shall We haven't stopped much since coming to London.

I could never do Home Service — that is service in London in the British Red Cross. I should have been home a year ago, if I hadn't gone abroad again. The life here is so stiff; our camp and barrack life is quite free and easy: no formalities comparatively speaking. I pity the war time girls here.

Your Daughter Fanny

I cannot write any more: I must write so many others.
Good Bye Mother: I am dying for a home meal:
See you very soon.

Your loving daughter Fannie.

AFTERWORD

To read the letters of Newfoundland's Great War VAD, Frances Cluett, is to experience, vicariously, the life and times of our men and women who went to the aid of Great Britain between 1914 and 1918.

From the fall of 1915, recruitment for Britain's fighting lines was in major crisis. Staffing needs for British military hospitals and transport lines (ambulances, hospital trains, and ships) had also reached crisis proportions. From October 1916, Frances Cluett of Belleoram, Fortune Bay, became an active witness to and an immediate recorder of the catastrophic events unfolding in Europe. In retrospect, she became an unofficial Newfoundland War correspondent.

Unbeknownst to Fanny, in October 1916, the prerequisite six-week training program for nursing probationers (VADs), including herself and seven other new recruits, had been truncated. So urgent was the need for nursing personnel both on the home front in Britain and on the war front in Europe, that she and her classmates completed the qualifying examinations in just four weeks.

In November 1916 Fanny Cluett was attached to the No. 4 Northern General Hospital, a military hospital, in Lincoln. On April 26, 1917, just five months after her arrival in England, she was en route to France. In the opening months of the War the transfer of such an inexperienced VAD to a battle front casualty hospital would have been unthinkable. Her rapid promotion and relocation to France underlines not only the medical crisis facing the War, but also speaks volumes about Fanny's competence as a nurse, her skill, courage, and commitment.

Her arrival at No. 10 British General Hospital at Rouen, France, occurred shortly after the Newfoundland Regiment's heavy losses in the fighting at Monchy in early April 1917. Through the six months that followed she experienced more horror than she had ever hoped to see. Then on November 26, the War struck her personally: her first cousin, 2nd Lieutenant Vincent Cluett, died of injuries sustained in fighting at Marcoing Masnières.

Fanny and Vince wrote to each other regularly and had always planned on meeting up in Paris, but his death ended that dream forever. It was a grievous loss for her and for all her family and friends back in Belleoram. She had hoped to visit his grave at Etaples Military Cemetery in France, to bring closure to that tragic event in her life, but was unable to make the necessary arrangements before her return to Newfoundland in 1920.

Frances Cluett's lengthy overseas experience is representative of all Newfoundland female veterans from World War I. Wherever there was a Newfoundland male in the military or naval forces of Great Britain during this War, more often than not there was a mother, a sister, a fiancée, a war bride, a widow, fulfilling the role of professional nurse, or VAD or ambulance driver. Fanny and her sisterhood volunteered "to bear their part, as important in degree as the actual taking up of arms." She was one of many Newfoundland women "who for brave men's lives . . . fought with death and dulled the sword." Fanny Cluett's heroic wartime life is cause for celebration.

August 2, 2014, is the 100th anniversary of the beginning of World War I. The definitive, unvarnished story of Newfoundland's men and women veterans of that War has yet to be compiled. It should and must, for the sake of decency, justice, education and remembrance, be published in the interim. Only then will we appreciate what happened not only in battle, but between battles. Only then will we know how much was given and appreciate what was lost to our then nation of Newfoundland.

In reading this volume of war letters, and in recognition of the Newfoundland men and women currently serving in conflicts on distant shores, remember Fanny Cluett and her youthful maturity, her courage, her strength, her endurance and, ultimately, her resiliency. For these characteristics symbolize Newfoundland itself.

Mary Philpott
July 2006

BIBLIOGRAPHY

Andrieux, J. P. *Prohibition and St. Pierre*. Lincoln, ON: W. F. Rannie, 1983.

Cramm, Richard. *The First Five Hundred*. New York: C. F. Williams, [1921].

Dominix, Arthur H. "History of Belleoram." Memorial University of Newfoundland, 1970. [unpublished].

Evans, Allen. *The Splendor of St. Jacques*. St. John's: Harry Cuff, 1981.

Fudge, John Marshall. *The Late Capt. J. M. Fudge: His Life Story as a Fisherman and Businessman*. Moncton, NB: Atlas Press, [1963].

Gallishaw, John. *Trenching at Gallipoli: The Personal Narrative of a Newfoundlander With the Ill-Fated Dardanelles Expedition*. Toronto: S. B. Gundy, 1916.

MacDermott, Hugh J. A. *MacDermott of Fortune Bay, as Told by Himself*. London: Hodder & Stroughton, [1938].

Nicholson, G. W. L. *The Fighting Newfoundlander*. St. John's: Government of Newfoundland, [1964].

O'Brien, Patricia. "The Newfoundland Patriotic Association: The Administration of the War Effort, 1914–1918." Master's thesis, Memorial University of Newfoundland, 1981. [unpublished].

Rannie, William F. *Saint Pierre and Miquelon*. Beamsville, ON: Rannie Publications, 1963.

Rompkey, William and Peter Rompkey. "Notes from an
      Interview with Margaret Rompkey." Ottawa, 1998.

Rusted, Nigel. *It's Devil Deep Down There*. St. John's: Creative
      Publishers, 1987.

Taylor, V. R. "The Community of Belleoram: Its Name and
      Origins" *Newfoundland Quarterly* 91 (Spring 1988):
      37–39.

ACKNOWLEDGEMENTS

Janice Marshall, who translated Frances Cluett's erratic hand-writing into a legible typescript, Kate Skipton, who undertook preliminary research for the annotations, Mary Cluett, Rev. Frank Cluett, John LaFosse, Olive Burdock, Dorothy Petite, Leah Taylor, Vince Taylor, Carolyn Morgan, and last, but by no means least, my wife, Carolyn.

WHR

Linda White, who expertly arranged and described the Frances Cluett papers, creating order out of havoc, upon their arrival at the Centre for Newfoundland Studies Archives (now Archives and Manuscripts Division), Queen Elizabeth II Library, Memorial University; Gail Weir, Anne Hart, Joan Ritcey, and all the other wonderful colleagues with whom I have had the pleasure to work at the archives over the past twenty years; Rev. Vernon Cluett, who lovingly preserved the letters, photographs and other materials, and donated them to the archives to ensure their safekeeping; Mary Philpott, who knows more than anyone else in the world about Newfoundland VADs, for agreeing to write the afterword; Ruby Cluett Kocurko who provided an important photograph; Garry and Margo Cranford and Dwayne LaFitte at Flanker Press for their professionalism, dedication, and understanding every time I wanted to make a change in the text; and to Adam Freake for the best cover design I have seen in years.

BGR

About the Editors

William H. Rompkey, PC, M.A., LL.D. (born May 13, 1936) is a Canadian politician. He was first elected to the Canadian House of Commons in the 1972 federal election as the Liberal member of Parliament (M.P.) for Grand Falls–White Bay–Labrador, the first of seven consecutive election victories. In 1995, Prime Minister Jean Chrétien appointed Rompkey to the Canadian Senate where he still serves. In 2001, he became government whip in the Senate and was deputy leader of the government in the Senate until February 2006. He is the author of *From the Coast to Far Inland* and *The Story of Labrador.*

Bert Riggs (born December 21, 1954) holds a B.A. and a B.Ed. from Memorial University and a masters in information studies from the University of Toronto. He has been an archivist at Memorial University since 1989 and currently is head of the Archives and Manuscripts Division at the university's Queen Elizabeth II Library. He writes a weekly column for the St. John's *Telegram*, is a bencher with the Law Society of Newfoundland and Labrador, and is chair of the board of the Resource Centre for the Arts, owners and operators of the LSPU Hall.